More Praise for *Doing the Right Thi*

D0255009

"Laura Stack is one of the brightest pro. content is useful. Her approach is practical. Her recommendations are right on. I recommend her work with conviction."
—**Nido R. Qubein, President, High Point University**

"If you're tired of all the business fables and want real-world coaching on getting more done, then this is the book for you."
—**Randy Gage, author of the *New York Times* bestseller *Risky Is the New Safe* and *Mad Genius***

"I hired Laura Stack personally six years ago. My staff and I were frazzled and felt overworked and out of control. Stack came to town and came to work and life has been better since. Rarely does a day go by that I don't think of one or two of the productive tips she teaches. Now, *Doing the Right Things Right* comes along and updates, refreshes, and adds a new perspective to the science of productivity and all that I thought I knew. Read this book so you too can 'manufacture' that time in your life that you need so you can go home early!"
—**Montague Boyd, CFP, forty-year financial advisor, Atlanta, Georgia**

"Laura Stack doesn't beat around the bush when it comes to productive advice—because that would waste time. Not a word's wasted here. Her examples are to the point, her advice concise, and the book itself surprisingly brief. If she were anyone else, I'd say she tried to cram too many topics into one book, but that's part of this book's utility—this book saves time and shelf space."
—**Jeremy Eaves, Director, People Services, DaVita Inc.**

"To be successful in business, you must make money, and time is money. The more time you can save, the more of it you can repurpose to higher-value activities. In *Doing the Right Things Right*, Laura Stack offers leaders a practical guide on doing their jobs efficiently and effectively."
—**Alex Doverspike, Director of Financial Services, Chick-fil-A, Inc.**

"Once again the 'right' thing to do is to read Laura's latest book, *Doing the Right Things Right*. Her time-saving productivity systems are vital to strong leadership of self or team. Her practical approach, coupled with a quarter century of teaching leaders, will help you succeed without the pain of mistakes."
—**Jeff Bettinger, Global Head of Talent Acquisition, Alcon**

"I love Laura's refreshingly practical perspective. No one really cares how many items you've crossed off your to-do list or how many hours you spend at the office. What matters is that you get the right things done—and that's what this no-nonsense little book will teach you to do."
—**Laura Vanderkam, author of** *I Know How She Does It*

"Laura Stack has taken the best ideas of Peter Drucker to a new level for the 21st century. This book shows you how to dramatically increase your efficiency, effectiveness, and results—faster than you ever thought possible."
—**Brian Tracy, author of** *Time Power* **and** *Eat That Frog!*

"I have never met a professional who provides so many immediately impactful solutions to navigating through this busy world and tough business environment. If you follow the concepts that Laura sculpts, you can gather insight into *where* you might improve your results, understand *why* you might be falling short in some areas, and find practical *ways* to improve both your work and your life."
—**Cathy Krause, Learning and Development Manager, MillerCoors**

"Execute today, plan for tomorrow, and invite the very best from your team. Sound compelling? Then add Laura Stack's latest book, *Doing the Right Things Right*, to the top of your reading list. There's no time to waste, so use her 3T Leadership Assessment and jump straight to the content that will help you most!"
—**Catherine Stewart, talent, culture, and organizational development consultant, H&R Block**

"More than a book, *Doing the Right Things Right* is a complete program in leadership efficiency and effectiveness. Offering a tool for analysis, online support, and resources for additional information, Laura Stack provides an exceptional straightforward model for organizational and personal productivity."
—**Karla R. Peters-Van Havel, PhD, COO, Institute for Management Studies**

"I'm a big fan of concise writing and straight talk, so I found Stack's *Doing the Right Things Right: How the Effective Executive Spends Time* right on the mark. Stack makes it easy for executives at all levels to be effective and efficient in twelve practical chapters."
—**Jennifer Colosimo, coauthor of** *Great Work, Great Career* **(with Stephen R. Covey) and former Vice President of Wisdom, DaVita Healthcare Partners**

DOING THE RIGHT THINGS RIGHT

Other Books by Laura Stack

*Execution IS the Strategy: How Leaders Achieve
Maximum Results in Minimum Time*

*What to Do When There's Too Much to Do: Reduce Tasks,
Increase Results, and Save 90 Minutes a Day*

*SuperCompetent: The Six Keys to
Perform at Your Productive Best*

*The Exhaustion Cure: Up Your Energy
from Low to Go in 21 Days*

*Find More Time: How to Get Things Done at Home,
Organize Your Life, and Feel Great About It*

*Leave the Office Earlier: How to Do More in
Less Time and Feel Great About It*

DOING THE **RIGHT** THINGS **RIGHT**

How the Effective Executive Spends Time

LAURA STACK

BK

Berrett–Koehler Publishers, Inc.
a BK Business book

Berrett-Koehler Publishers, Inc.
1333 Broadway, Suite 1000
Oakland, CA 94612-1921
Tel: (510) 817-2277   Fax: (510) 817-2278   www.bkconnection.com

Ordering Information

Quantity sales. Special discounts are available on quantity purchases by corporations, associations, and others. For details, contact the "Special Sales Department" at the Berrett-Koehler address above.

Individual sales. Berrett-Koehler publications are available through most bookstores. They can also be ordered directly from Berrett-Koehler: Tel: (800) 929-2929; Fax: (802) 864-7626; www.bkconnection.com

Orders for college textbook/course adoption use. Please contact Berrett-Koehler: Tel: (800) 929-2929; Fax: (802) 864-7626.

Orders by U.S. trade bookstores and wholesalers. Please contact Ingram Publisher Services, Tel: (800) 509-4887; Fax: (800) 838-1149; E-mail: customer.service@ingrampublisherservices.com; or visit www.ingrampublisherservices.com/Ordering for details about electronic ordering.

Berrett-Koehler and the BK logo are registered trademarks of Berrett-Koehler Publishers, Inc.

Printed in the United States of America

Berrett-Koehler books are printed on long-lasting acid-free paper. When it is available, we choose paper that has been manufactured by environmentally responsible processes. These may include using trees grown in sustainable forests, incorporating recycled paper, minimizing chlorine in bleaching, or recycling the energy produced at the paper mill.

Library of Congress Cataloging-in-Publication Data
Names: Stack, Laura.
Title: Doing the right things right : how the effective executive spends time / Laura Stack.
Description: First Edition. | Oakland : Berrett-Koehler Publishers, 2015. |
   Includes bibliographical references.
Identifiers: LCCN 2015036710 | ISBN 9781626565661 (pbk.)
Subjects: LCSH: Executive ability. | Strategic planning. | Management.
Classification: LCC HD38.2 .S73 2015 | DDC 658.4/093—dc23
LC record available at http://lccn.loc.gov/2015036710

First Edition
20 19 18 17 16   10 9 8 7 6 5 4 3 2 1

Produced by Wilsted & Taylor Publishing Services
Cover and interior design: Nancy Koerner

To Kathy Cooperman,
my first mentor,
who took me under her wing
25 years ago

You taught the first
time management seminar
I ever attended.

I still use the principles you taught me.

Thank you.

CONTENTS

FOREWORD

My intention in writing this foreword is to introduce you to the book *Doing the Right Things Right: How the Effective Executive Spends Time* by Laura Stack, aka The Productivity Pro®. But above and beyond a simple introduction, I'm going to tell you why reading this book is one of the "rightest" things you can do for yourself.

For you to understand why I can make such a claim and why it matters, you have to understand where I'm coming from.

Recently, I received an email from Neal Maillet, one of my early editors, announcing that he was editing a new book. There's nothing unusual about that; it's what editors do. But this one had him excited. He insisted that I consider writing the foreword.

I have a soft spot for former editors, but I didn't want to commit without seeing the manuscript first. I told him I would read the book and then make my decision. He sent me the entire manuscript right away. I was immediately hooked.

As Laura explains in her preface, her book was inspired by Peter Drucker's *The Effective Executive*. Drucker is nothing less than the Father of Modern Management, and this was one of his classics, written in the mid-1960s. Laura describes it as her favorite book, and I have no difficulty understanding why that's so.

You see, Peter Drucker was a true genius. There are Drucker Societies today in more than nineteen countries, still studying and analyzing his thirty-nine books and hundreds of articles and speeches ten years after his death. I was the first to receive my PhD at Drucker's hands, and I later founded the California Institute of Advanced Management (CIAM), to offer an affordable MBA in Executive Management and Entrepreneurship based on the principles and values of Peter Drucker. In addition, I write a syndicated column on Drucker, and my last four books are all about Drucker and his ideas.

I devoured Laura's book—and what a feast it was! Understand, Drucker was the first scholar to differentiate management and leadership, and this difference goes a long way toward explaining both Peter's and Laura's book titles. "Management," Peter said, "is about doing things right—leadership is about doing the right things." He went on to write that the latter was critical, and that while doing things right meant efficiency, doing the right things was about being effective.

Thus, *The Effective Executive*. Of course, we'd like managers to be both efficient *and* effective, because, as Laura points out and Drucker proclaimed, nothing is worse than spending time, effort, and money in doing the wrong things with 100 percent efficiency. So Laura set herself the task of showing us how *To Do the Right Things Right*. She succeeds wonderfully.

Laura does far more, actually. Without a doubt, Drucker's genius was in showing us *what* to do. Rarely, however, did he tell us *how* or suggest ways to carry out his recommendations and insights. Laura does. In just over 50,000 words, she goes nonstop with hundreds of ways, steps, and checklists to implement Drucker's ideas. If you don't get at least a couple of million-dollar ideas on every page, you aren't paying attention. The breadth of coverage is more than impressive—it is amazing.

Laura categorizes the three areas where leaders spend their time into what she calls "The Three Ts": Thinking Strategically, Team Focus, and Tactical Work. Then, with four principles in each, she covers everything about each from Action to Vision, and everything in between and back again. Moreover, she illustrates everything with specific examples so you know exactly what she is talking about and exactly how to apply her ideas.

You'll enjoy and profit from her book. I know I did.

—*Bill Cohen, PhD*
Major General, USAF, Ret.;
President, California Institute
of Advanced Management

This book pays homage to a man I consider one of my chief mentors and kindred spirits, though I never actually had the pleasure of studying or working with him.

When I was a business student in the late 1980s, I fell in love with Peter F. Drucker's book *The Effective Executive: The Definitive Guide to Getting the Right Things Done*. It delivers a huge amount of useful, real-world information in fewer than two hundred pages. It's still my favorite business book of all time, and I learn something new every time I read it.

Drucker published the first edition of *The Effective Executive* in 1967. While the book has weathered the years well, some of the concepts are a bit dated, particularly with today's technology and social customs. Drucker doesn't cover the electronics revolution that swept the business world in the 1980s, even in later editions; and in this book, executives are men and women are secretaries. I don't believe he intended to be sexist, however, because the secretarial pool was the main foothold women had in business then.

Regardless, I believe the time is right to update Drucker's concepts for the twenty-first century. *Doing the Right Things Right: How the Effective Executive Spends Time* focuses on time management strategies that today's executives can use to quickly obtain profitable, productive results by managing the intersection of two critical dimensions: effectiveness and efficiency. The impact of technology plays an important part in the discussions outlined here, and that I have included gender equality goes without saying.

I don't mean to replace Drucker's work in any sense, nor could I. Let me emphasize that this is NOT an attempt to rewrite Drucker's classic. However, I do hope that *Doing the Right Things Right* will stand as a companion to Drucker's work, an addition that directly addresses how the role of the effective executive has changed in the almost half-century since Drucker penned the first edition of his groundbreaking book *The Effective Executive*.

I'm humbled by the opportunity to attempt it.

DOING THE RIGHT THINGS RIGHT

INTRODUCTION

There is nothing so useless
as doing efficiently that which
should not be done at all.

—PETER F. DRUCKER

It's not surprising that *The Effective Executive* is one of the most widely read business books in the world. A brief, straightforward book on how an executive can best serve his or her organization, it has, after all, been available continuously for just shy of fifty years. I know I'm not alone in considering it my favorite and most instructive business book.

In *The Effective Executive*, Peter Drucker provides what he promises in the subtitle: a definitive guide to getting the right things done, complete with all the things an effective executive must do to help keep his or her organization afloat. He explains the "why" and the "what to do" in a superlative manner—as always. If the book has a flaw, however, it's in not examining the "how."

How does the modern executive—a somewhat different animal from the executive Drucker defined in 1967—do the

1

job both effectively *and* efficiently? How does the executive at any level mine that intersection of effectiveness and efficiency to get the right things done *right*?

Let's start with the key definitions. Drucker's book distinguishes between being effective and efficient. Here's how I differentiate the two terms:

> ***Effectiveness*** refers to successfully producing the expected or desired result; it's the degree to which you achieve your objectives, solve problems, and realize profits. In business, effectiveness is summed up by "doing the right things."

> ***Efficiency*** is the accomplishment of a job with the minimum expenditure of time, effort, and cost—the shortest distance between a goal and a checkmark. In business, efficiency is summed up by "doing things right."

Alone, effectiveness isn't enough to distinguish a good executive, since anyone with the right training or a good manual can do the right things. So can a robot. When effectiveness lacks efficiency, it's often unproductive. A task that should take four months to complete can end up taking fourteen. Additionally, efficiency without effectiveness can go devastatingly wrong. It doesn't matter how well your team climbs Mount Everest if your intention was to climb the Matterhorn.

I'm sure you'd agree that executives should work to be not only effective but also efficient. *Doing the Right Things Right* combines Effectiveness (doing the right things) with Efficiency (doing things right) to yield the most profitable AND quickest route a leader can take to execute goals. Leaders manage time most productively at the intersection of effectiveness and efficiency. Therefore, once you know you're spending time on the *right* things, you then focus on doing them *right*.

WHO IS AN EXECUTIVE?

In today's business vernacular, we usually assume an executive is someone in a senior leadership position. However, the dictionary defines an executive as "a person or group appointed and given the responsibility to manage the affairs of an organization, and the authority to make decisions within specified boundaries."

In reality, an executive is *someone who executes*—almost anyone with the authority to make significant decisions and whose time is spent producing value and/or managing people for the benefit of the organization. An executive might be an emerging leader, a front-line supervisor, a middle manager, a senior leader, or even an individual contributor who hasn't received a title.

In *The Effective Executive*, Drucker outlines five effectiveness practices, or what he refers to as "habits of the mind," for executives to follow, which I summarize as:

- Understand and control where time goes.

- Focus on results.

- Build on strengths.

- Prioritize tasks.

- Make effective decisions.

THE EFFECTIVE AND EFFICIENT EXECUTIVE

To be both effective and efficient, today's leaders should follow twelve practices (see facing chart). Some of these practices were not as germane in Drucker's time as they are now, or they were considered too obvious to state explicitly. However, priorities have changed over the decades, and sometimes even the obvious must be spelled out.

These twelve practices, which supplement Drucker's work and correspond to the twelve chapters of this book, describe how to do the right things the right way. They are up to speed for our modern times, where flexibility, agility, and on-the-spot, in-the-moment execution rule. Today, an executive not only must do the right things but also must carefully ensure he or she does the right things *right*, wasting as little time as possible in the process.

THE 3T LEADERSHIP MODEL

What leaders actually "do" during the day and where they spend their time can be grouped into three leadership activities that I call the "3T Leadership" roles. These three activities (Strategic Thinking, Team Focus, and Tactical Work) also describe the three parts of this book. As shorthand, I'll refer to these 3Ts as THINK, TEAM, and TACTICS. The 3Ts are the chief time management roles for leaders:

STRATEGIC *THINKING*

Acting as the organizational strategist
who focuses on business goals.
The executive monitors the big picture
and makes sure the team efforts reinforce
the company's goals.

DOING THE RIGHT THINGS RIGHT

1 GOALS
Align strategy and objectives

2 CHANGE
Embrace innovation and adaptability

3 COMMUNICATION
Share mission, vision, and expectations

4 DECISION-MAKING
Resolve and execute decisions promptly

5 ENVIRONMENT
Build an open team culture

6 PERFORMANCE
Forge a results-oriented team

7 MOTIVATION
Harness creativity and loyalty

8 GROWTH
Emphasize continuous improvement

9 VALUE
Focus on high-impact activities

10 TECHNOLOGY
Master data handling and workflow

11 AGILITY
Maximize speed and flexibility

12 BALANCE
Sustain personal health and mental acuity

TEAM *FOCUS*

Serving as the conscientious leader who
focuses on employee productivity.
The executive builds and maintains an
effective, productive team as the first step
toward high performance.

TACTICAL *WORK*

Being the productive performer who
focuses on task completion.
The executive completes his or her
individual duties and carries out any
day-to-day, operational activities.

The "3T Leadership Model" on the facing page not only
aptly summarizes the 3T Leadership Roles with their individual components and associated concepts, but it also summarizes
the content of this book. THINK, TEAM, and TACTICS are
found at the center of the chart. The twelve chapter titles (the
twelve practices for doing the right things) radiate out from
the center. Attached to each title are three themes discussed in
that chapter.

In general, as an executive moves up the leadership ladder,
the percentage of time spent in each category tends to shift,
becoming less tactical and more strategic. This focus may also
vary according to the executive's position or immediate project needs. You may not be content with the current mix of
your time in these three areas. Perhaps you feel you spend too
much time "in the weeds," dealing with day-to-day operational issues, and not enough time with your team. Or perhaps
you spend too much time managing your team's work and

The 3T Leadership Model

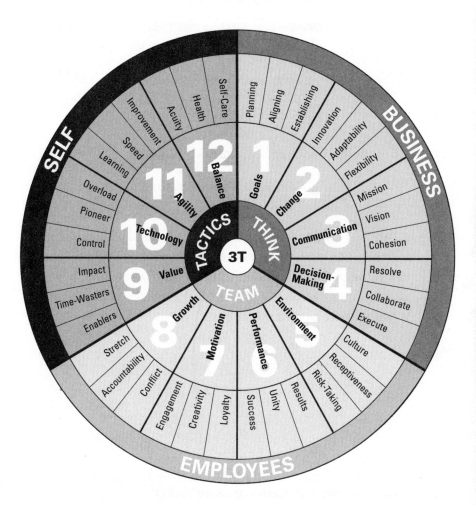

The 3T Leadership Roles with their individual practices and associated concepts.

not enough time focused on strategic activities. With the area requiring the largest investment of time listed first, here's a typical breakdown of the 3Ts for various leadership levels:

Senior Leadership (VP/C-Suite)
1. Think   2. Team   3. Tactics

Leadership Team (Director)
1. Team   2. Think   3. Tactics

Manager
1. Team   2. Tactics   3. Think

Individual Contributor
1. Tactics   2. Team   3. Think

Are you starting to see that where you spend your time *now* isn't necessarily where you *should* be spending your time? You can get started by taking the 3T Leadership Assessment. It will provide insight into your current level of efficient effectiveness as you prepare to read this book.

▶▶ **START DOING THE RIGHT THINGS RIGHT**
Keep the momentum going and continue to develop your time management skills after reading this book! Visit **www.3TLeadership.com** for free related resources, including a personal journal to take notes as you read, a discussion guide to share with your leadership team, and video lessons to review key learning points.

THE 3T
LEADERSHIP
ASSESSMENT

Strategy execution is becoming more common at all levels
within the white-collar business hierarchy, making more of
us *de facto* executives. Good execution requires you to do the
right things right: that is, you have to be both efficient and
effective in completing your tasks or meeting your objectives.
The assessment is divided into sections that follow the book's
parts and chapters. Each question has a focus highlighted in
bold and repeated in the scoring section.

Before you start, I recommend photocopying the assessment, rather than marking your answers in the book itself.
That way, you can come back and retake the assessment as
your working conditions change and your career advances.
Or you can go to www.3TLeadership.com to take the
assessment online. After you take the assessment, use the
Score Sheet at the end to analyze your scores further.

TAKING THE ASSESSMENT

For each question, begin by asking yourself "To what extent
do I...", and then answer it using the following scale:

> 1 = to no extent
> 2 = to a small extent
> 3 = to some extent
> 4 = to a considerable extent
> 5 = to a great extent

PART 1: STRATEGIC THINKING

1. Goals
Align Strategy and Objectives

1. Understand our overall strategic **planning** process from beginning to end?

   1   2   3   4   5

2. Work toward actively **aligning** our team and individual goals with organizational goals?

   1   2   3   4   5

3. Focus on **establishing** team goals and encouraging my team to take ownership of them?

   1   2   3   4   5

   GOALS SUBTOTAL: _____

2. Change
Embrace Innovation and Adaptability

4. Foster **innovation** and continually nurture and implement new ideas?

   1   2   3   4   5

5. Encourage faster **adaptability** to the agile business environment?

   1   2   3   4   5

6. Increase **flexibility** and embrace chaos during times of change?

   1   2   3   4   5

   CHANGE SUBTOTAL: _____

3. Communication
Share Mission, Vision, and Ideas

7. Communicate our **mission** in straightforward terms and ensure my team's understanding?

   1   2   3   4   5

8. Promote my **vision** to my peers and upper management clearly?

   1   2   3   4   5

9. Create **cohesion** and present a united front when I sell new initiatives to senior leaders?

   1   2   3   4   5

   COMMUNICATION SUBTOTAL: _____

4. Decision-Making
Resolve and Execute Decisions Promptly

10. **Resolve** indecision quickly?

    1   2   3   4   5

11. **Collaborate** and emphasize the value of teamwork?

    1   2   3   4   5

12. Avoid procrastination, encouraging the team to **execute** and implement strategy immediately?

    1   2   3   4   5

    DECISION-MAKING SUBTOTAL: _____

PART II: TEAM FOCUS

5. Environment
Build an Open Team Culture

13. Create a **culture** of team efficiency by simplifying workflow and improving processes?

                    1   2   3   4   5

14. Encourage team **receptiveness** toward urgency, nimbleness, and swift execution?

                    1   2   3   4   5

15. Reward **risk-taking** and challenge my team to think creatively?

                    1   2   3   4   5

ENVIRONMENT SUBTOTAL: _____

6. Performance
Forge a Results-Oriented Team

16. Teach my team that **results** matter first, emphasizing substance over style?

                    1   2   3   4   5

17. Encourage team **unity** and mediate clashes?

                    1   2   3   4   5

18. Build on strengths and reduce weaknesses to create greater team **success**?

                    1   2   3   4   5

PERFORMANCE SUBTOTAL: _____

7. Motivation
Harness Creativity and Loyalty

19. Understand and implement employee **engagement** techniques?

          1   2   3   4   5

20. Encourage **creativity** and resourcefulness on my team?

          1   2   3   4   5

21. Maximize **loyalty**, treating my team members with respect, trust, and gratitude?

          1   2   3   4   5

MOTIVATION SUBTOTAL: _____

8. Growth
Emphasize Continuous Improvement

22. **Stretch** my team's abilities by encouraging them to grow?

          1   2   3   4   5

23. Emphasize **accountability** and expect team members to take responsibility for their needs, shortcomings, and errors?

          1   2   3   4   5

24. Encourage healthy **conflict** on my team?

          1   2   3   4   5

GROWTH SUBTOTAL: _____

PART III: TACTICAL WORK

9. Value
Focus on High-Impact Activities

25. Place a high value on my time and maximize my personal **impact**?

    1   2   3   4   5

26. Clear **time-wasters** for my team, making it easier for everyone to be productive?

    1   2   3   4   5

27. Add productivity **enablers** to my team, such as by saying no and reducing wasted time in meetings?

    1   2   3   4   5

VALUE SUBTOTAL: _____

10. Technology
Master Data Handling and Workflow

28. Deal effectively with information **overload** and efficiently handle workflow?

    1   2   3   4   5

29. **Pioneer** new technology?

    1   2   3   4   5

30. Establish tight **control** over my technology without letting it control me?

    1   2   3   4   5

TECHNOLOGY SUBTOTAL: _____

11. Agility
Maximize Speed and Flexibility

31. Stress **improvement** by focusing on genuine, quantifiable results?

                1   2   3   4   5

22. Emphasize **speed** when responding to unexpected situations?

                1   2   3   4   5

33. Use consistent training and **learning** opportunities to stay ahead of the changes in my field?

                1   2   3   4   5

AGILITY SUBTOTAL: _____

12. Balance
Sustain Your Physical and Mental Health

34. Practice personal **self-care** and relaxation on a regular basis?

                1   2   3   4   5

35. Maintain my personal **health**?

                1   2   3   4   5

36. Work to sharpen my mental **acuity** and intelligence?

                1   2   3   4   5

BALANCE SUBTOTAL: _____

THE 3T LEADERSHIP SCORE SHEET

Copy your subtotals from the previous sections and add them up to find your grand total. See the key below to interpret your score.

PART I. STRATEGIC THINKING

1. Goals   SUBTOTAL _____

2. Change   SUBTOTAL _____

3. Communication   SUBTOTAL _____

4. Decision-Making   SUBTOTAL _____

                                  PART I TOTAL _____

PART II. TEAM FOCUS

5. Environment   SUBTOTAL _____

6. Performance   SUBTOTAL _____

7. Motivation   SUBTOTAL _____

8. Growth   SUBTOTAL _____

                                  PART II TOTAL _____

PART III. TACTICAL WORK

9. Value   SUBTOTAL _____

10. Technology   SUBTOTAL _____

11. Agility   SUBTOTAL _____

12. Balance   SUBTOTAL _____

                                  PART III TOTAL _____

        GRAND TOTAL (ADD PARTS I, II, III TOTALS): _____

SCORING

151–180: **Congratulations!** You have a deep understanding of what it takes to be an efficient, effective modern executive and how to help your team members maximize their productivity. At most, all you need to do is fine-tune a bit. Keep up the good work!

121–150: **You need a few tweaks here and there**. You're on the right track! Strive to improve any question where you gave yourself less than a "5." Give yourself credit for what you do well. Acknowledge where you can improve to become an even better executive.

91–120: **Average**. You're in the middle of the bell curve. You're not the worst, and you're not the best. Work on kicking your efforts toward achieving effective, efficient execution up a notch, so you can perform at a higher level and produce greater results. For twelve weeks, focus on one of the twelve chapters each week and work to improve your weak areas and build on your strengths.

61–90: **Major overhaul required**. Get serious about changing the way you handle your team and projects. Are you efficient but ineffective, or effective but inefficient? Without neglecting your area of strength, start focusing on improving your area of weakness. Stop working so hard on the wrong things or doing the right things wrong—whichever happens to be the case. Break your weaknesses down into subcategories, based on the ones in the assessment above. Work on one item on this list over the course of several months until you systematically improve your competence level.

36–60: **Danger**! You're both ineffective and inefficient. Your leadership productivity skills need a jumpstart *fast*! Both your job and your organization's future may depend on it, so start working hard on doing the right things the right way right now.

HOW TO USE YOUR SCORES

Comparing scores on each part of this assessment will help you determine which of the 3Ts is the weakest link in your executive process. I've divided the assessment as I have so that within each part, you can delve deeper by comparing the chapter subtotals, thereby better understanding in which topics you've expressed a weakness. Even more useful is looking at the individual quiz items with the lowest scores; in fact, those represent your best places to start working. Regard this as a bottom-up method of continuous improvement.

As you study each chapter (especially those in which you've scored poorly), think about how you can improve your process. If your weakest of the 3Ts is Team, where do you face your greatest challenges: in Environment, Performance, Motivation, or Growth? If you've marked a full slate of 5s except in the Performance chapter (chapter 6) where you drop to 4 on Results, 2 on Unity, and 1 on Success, then your scores mark a clear line of action. Start with working on improving your team's success, followed by encouraging team unity.

Make a sincere effort to weld your team together as an effective, productive unit, providing the training and education needed to improve their return on investment as both individuals and a team. Aim to increase their performance all around. Do the same for yourself.

Once you're happy with your new results, move on to another unsatisfactory function and work on bringing it up to par. While I would normally tell you to focus on improving what you're already good at—i.e., pushing your scores from good to great rather than wasting time on things you don't do well—the functions I discuss in this book represent exceptions to that rule. They're so fundamental that they require the highest level of competence you can bring to bear. That way, you and your team can strategically execute on the spot so automatically that you ensure your survival in an increasingly difficult business world.

As you successfully put new concepts into play, retake the assessment to determine how much you've improved. You may not even recognize that original *you* a year from now!

Don't forget to visit www.3TLeadership.com for additional tools and information to supplement this book.

PART I

STRATEGIC **THINKING**

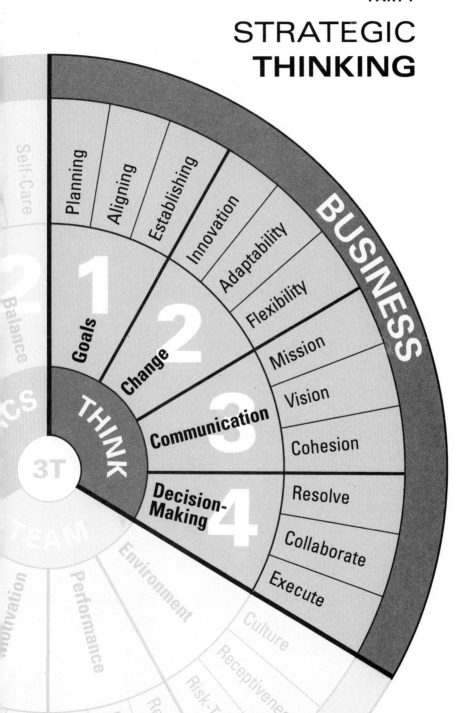

Self-Care

Balance

3T

THINK

TEAM

Planning

Aligning

Establishing

Innovation

Adaptability

Flexibility

Mission

Vision

Cohesion

Resolve

Collaborate

Execute

BUSINESS

1

Goals

2

Change

3

Communication

4

Decision-Making

Performance

Environment

Culture

Receptiveness

Risk-Taking

Results

Strategic thinking boils down to one simple question:
What is the desired outcome?

The answer to that question helps an executive drive
organizational strategy through various ways to:

- Maximize results in minimal time.
- Maintain a bird's-eye view of the big picture.
- Ensure the team aligns its goals with those of the
  organization.

As a leader, you have to regularly set aside time for strategic
thinking, so you can take your team from start to finish
with the least interference along the way. My clients tell me,
"We want our employees to be strategic enablers of business." I tell them, "Well, then you have to give them time
to be strategic." As an executive, you must *create* the time to
think strategically—it won't magically materialize.

This makes sense and it's easy to say, but it begs this question: what exactly *is* strategic thinking in the first place?

THE COMPONENTS OF STRATEGIC THINKING

Although strategic thinking varies from one team or organization to another, it generally includes these characteristics:

- It focuses on group needs.
- It leverages existing organizational structure and seeks to improve upon it.
- It's cross-functional, presuming and requiring cooperation between groups.
- It has long-term, far-reaching effects.
- It considers what tactics can best be used to accomplish the desired outcome.

APPLYING STRATEGIC THINKING

Strategic thinking can be difficult to apply when circumstances—and sometimes people—seem determined to crush it. In addition to dealing with market forces and good old-fashioned competition, you may have to adroitly cope with crises over which you have no control.

Your goals tie together all the disparate members of a team, as well as the strategies that apply both individually and collectively. Goals set a course—a benchmark for the team to shoot for. In a sense, goals are promises to our teams and ourselves, dreams with deadlines that tweak our performance upward. The great thing about goals is that it's as easy to think big as it is to think small. Thinking big not only tests our reach and abilities; it also stretches our mental boundaries.

By its very nature, strategic thinking requires you to learn to make the best decisions you can as quickly as possible, boosting innovation and flexibility, helping your team adapt to circumstances as they change.

Just as importantly, you have to be able to communicate those adaptations to all involved: to communicate the new mission, to promote your vision, and to sell teamwork in a way that gets people to take notice.

Like the captain of a ship, you should always consult with your officers before making a decision, taking their viewpoints and suggestions into account. But the decisions are ultimately yours, and you must make them. If you don't, circumstances will make your decisions for you.

Once you've made a decision, you and your team have to execute immediately—on the spot if necessary.

REMEMBER

Executives *execute*. No one cares how many hours you spend at work and how many items you check off your to-do list. Execution and results are all that really matter in any business. And don't assume you don't qualify as an executive. An executive can be a front-line manager, an up-and-coming star, a programmer who institutes a productive change in a system or process . . . *anyone* who is responsible for results.

Planning

Aligning

Establishing

STRATEGIC THINKING

1

GOALS

Align Strategy and Objectives

If your team lacks clear goals, it may as well be a drunken octopus on roller skates. You'll get just as far. To be efficient and effective, you must set team goals, align them actively with organizational goals, and communicate them to your team.

You'll also need to regularly reevaluate your progress to ensure you're on the right path. If you're not already doing so, consider what course corrections might better serve you. "Strategic planning and goal setting should be linked," advises Janie Wade, Senior Vice President of Finance for Baylor Scott & White Health. "Everyone on the team should have goals that support the plan and each other. But the plans and the goals have to leave room for the unexpected opportunities that develop."

Goals also boost team productivity because they sow seeds of hope. They give your team something to strive for, especially if they're coupled with a positive, nonpunitive environment where you provide valuable feedback on a regular basis. Goals establish promises that you and your team can work toward as you fine-tune performance and boost productivity.

PLANNING: THE EXECUTION CONTINUUM

The first step in goal setting is to take a good, hard look at your organizational goals. Your personal and team goals should *always* contribute to or support the organization's overall goals. It's not necessarily easy to achieve alignment, and it's far too easy to drift off course once you have. But it is absolutely crucial to maintain your alignment, or the tactics you execute may be skewed from or entirely useless toward those goals. To keep that from happening, let's look at a basic formula that will help bring you on course and keep you there.

Logical, Strategic Execution

As with so many other things, business has borrowed the concepts of strategy and tactics from military and games theory. Yet researchers regard them as discrete, if interrelated, topics, and confusingly, often interchangeable terms. And when business still moved at human speed, we could afford to consider them separately. But in this electronics era, we no longer can.

In a previous book, *Execution IS the Strategy*, I focused on strategic execution itself, and described how today, we need to perceive strategy and tactics as what they truly are: points on an Execution Continuum. That continuum begins with an organization's core values, which represent the organization's bedrock, the foundational beliefs upon which its founders built it. Consider some Jewish-owned businesses, which close on Saturday—the Jewish Sabbath. Or some founded upon Christian values, which close on Sunday.

A mission statement builds on the core values and succinctly describes what a company does to achieve its vision, i.e., its ultimate purpose for existing. Vision and mission are incomplete without each other. For example, the National Speakers Association (NSA), of which I was president in 2011–2012, has as its vision, "Every expert who presents content to an audience through the spoken word for a fee belongs to NSA." Its mission is stated as, "NSA is the leading source for education, community, and entrepreneurial business knowledge needed to be successful in the speaking profession."

Mission and vision tell us where an organization wants to go; strategy and tactics are the means by which we get there. Strategic objectives feed the operational strategies of an organization and break down into departmental goals and individual performance objectives. Tactics achieve these goals, and resulting action items are executed.

Back to Basics

Strategy tends to fall into place more easily when it's built on mission, vision, and values—which, in turn, makes it easier to determine corresponding goals and tactics. Effective leaders hitch themselves to the organization's star and align team and personal goals with the organization's. Then they determine the most efficient ways to advance together.

ALIGNING YOUR TEAM

The effective, efficient executive uses alignment to strengthen the team—not only to shape its destiny but also to emphasize the mission and sow the seeds of hope for a better, more productive future. As we've already seen, goal setting begins in the soil of core values and is strengthened by the fertilizer of mission and vision. The outcomes are the harvest you reap.

Brenda Knowles, Vice President of Marketing at Shaw Industries, a flooring provider in Georgia, recently told me:

> Our strategic planning process and management meetings ensure that managers are clear on the company's growth strategy. With that strategic framework, we empower each of the business areas to bring forth recommendations for how to best meet customer needs and anticipate other market forces. This allows us to continue to innovate to ensure we're meeting and exceeding customer expectations and continually improving our products, processes, and services.
>
> So, I'd say my approach is one of including the team in the process, giving them the big picture and the guardrails, if you will, and relying upon their key strengths, insights into the company, and into our customers' business to help propel us forward. It's about empowerment and accountability.

Amen to that. How do you achieve such alignment?

Steps to Success

Getting strong-minded, independent people to work together on one objective can be like herding cats. But when they see how excited and personally committed you are to the goals, they'll be more likely to take ownership and put in the effort required to make their goals a reality. The following tips can strengthen your team's alignment:

1 **EMPHASIZE CORE VALUES.** Remind your team exactly where the organization is coming from and where it needs to go. Help them tie the mission/vision to the tasks they complete every day, since often this isn't apparent.

What happens when an organization loses track of its core values? Anything from a minor stumble to a complete meltdown. Back in 2001, energy company Enron self-destructed in a scandal that still amazes those who witnessed it. Despite the core values literally carved into the façade of its Houston headquarters—Respect, Integrity, Communication, and Excellence—top executives focused on feathering their own nests and defrauding stakeholders to the tune of billions of dollars.

2 **EMPHASIZE BOTH INDIVIDUAL CONTRIBUTIONS AND TEAM EFFORT.** I can't say it often enough: if you want to engage and empower your employees, tell each of them why their work matters and how it moves the organization forward. Otherwise, why should they ever look beyond the next paycheck? That said, you increase your productivity by an order of magnitude if everyone interlocks as a solid team.

Where do your team members feel lost? Where is more training needed? Encourage your team members to examine their daily work and help them fill in the blanks where they can't translate goals into operations. Urge them to ask for what they need to be more valuable to the marketplace, the organization, and the team.

3 **FOCUS ON A FEW MAJOR GOALS.** Rather than dividing your attention between twenty goals and doing none of them well, pick one to three goals and execute them brilliantly. Multitasking works no better for team achievement

than it does for individual productivity; you're better off
single-tasking in a fierce, focused way.

Break big goals into manageable pieces. This keeps more
complex goals from overwhelming your team. Each subgoal
builds on the previous one, right up the ladder.

4 **CELEBRATE WHEN YOU ACHIEVE A GOAL.** Don't just
robotically move from one project to the next. When
your team reaches a major milestone, have a party, give out
gift cards, or take everyone to lunch as a reward for hitting
that goal. Immediate gratification adds to the delayed gratification you'll receive when the entire project is complete.
Once you achieve and celebrate a goal, begin anew! Don't
rest on your laurels too long, or your team members might
get bored and lose their edge.

Stepping Up to the Plate

As the caterpillar told Alice in Wonderland in Lewis Carroll's
book, "If you do not know where you are going, any road
will get you there." You can't be like dandelion fluff, going
wherever the wind takes you. Destiny isn't a matter of *chance*;
it's a matter of *choice*. So shape your team to succeed and push
forward with a flexible methodology that gets you ahead and
keeps you there.

ESTABLISHING PRODUCTIVE AND RELIABLE GOALS

Goals tie together all the other factors crucial to modern business success: flexibility, agility, engagement, empowerment,
hard work, self-discipline, teamwork, cross-functionality, you
name it. They shape attention and provide direction in an increasingly chaotic world.

Political theorist Hannah Arendt once wrote, "Promises are the uniquely human way of ordering the future, making it predictable and reliable to the extent that this is humanly possible." Goals are a species of promise, and they apply to corporate teams as much as they do to any other human endeavor.

Setting Goals as a Team

Some of your team members will have a better understanding of goal-setting than others, so it's up to you to make sure they all stay on the same wavelength. Here's how:

1 **START WITH INDIVIDUAL TEAM MEMBERS.** You'll find it easier to establish team goals if individual members also have personal goals to reach for. Chris might want to make $150,000 annually by the time he's thirty-five, while Jane may prefer to move up the management ladder toward CFO. As you learn your team members' personal and professional development goals, help them find ways to weave those goals into the general goal-fabric of both team and organization.

2 **SET REASONABLE GOALS.** Whether it involves finishing a particular project or improving overall performance, provide your team with reasonable goals that include time-based milestones and objectives. Show them how they can increase their productivity over the next year or so, and communicate the plan clearly. Your team may surpass your expectations.

Precision counts: Tell your people precisely what they need to do to move everyone forward. The more detailed you are, the easier it is for them to engage. "Try harder" and

"Do your best" don't work nearly as well as "We need to improve output by 15 percent," "Each person needs to send twenty-five prospecting emails a day," or "Let's finish this project by next Friday."

3 **ENSURE A SUPPORTIVE, PRODUCTIVE WORKING ENVIRONMENT.** Invite open discussion and sharing of resources. Make sure that when someone is ill or a position is open, you have enough overlap in skill sets to fill in the blanks while you're short-staffed. Continually ask people how they think productivity can be improved. Getting people's input empowers them to participate, so meet with your team and brainstorm. They may have some innovative or easily implemented ideas to contribute, perhaps something as simple as issuing everyone an iPad, and these ideas will give them an opportunity to shine.

4 **CLEAR THE WAY TO THE TARGET—AND GIVE YOUR TEAM SOMETHING TO SHOOT FOR.** As the leader, you're also a facilitator. You not only have to clarify what the goals are and how to get there, but you'll also need to help blaze a trail. The quicker your team reaches one goal, the quicker they can move to the next—and the more productive they'll be.

In addition to providing the target itself, motivate your employees in positive ways—from offering bonuses to helping them climb the corporate ladder. Explain the rewards system and follow it meticulously, without favoritism. If your team can't trust you to keep your side of the bargain, why should they bother reaching for the goals?

5 **TRACK YOUR TEAM'S PRODUCTIVITY AND PROVIDE MEANINGFUL FEEDBACK.** You can't manage what you can't measure. Keep an eye on your team deliverables and overall production using Key Performance Indicators (KPIs), timesheet software, or scoreboard programs such as Kaptasystems.com or i-nexus.com. That way, you'll more easily see who needs help and who already pushes their productivity through the roof. Once you have that information in hand, you can provide meaningful feedback that includes specific growth ideas.

Purposeful Productivity

Good leaders give of themselves. Employees want someone to prepare the path for them, be there when they need them, and guide them along the way. They want you to actually *lead*. When you sincerely demonstrate compassion for your team, care about their futures, and hold everyone to their promises—including yourself—they'll follow you to the ends of the earth.

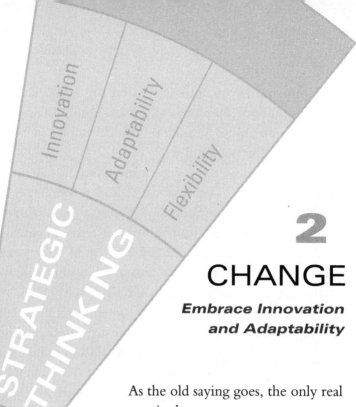

Innovation

Adaptability

Flexibility

STRATEGIC THINKING

2

CHANGE

Embrace Innovation and Adaptability

As the old saying goes, the only real constant is change.

Modern leadership involves more than just telling people what to do. Because you're responsible for helping the company stay profitable, you have no choice but to embrace change. This keeps your team functional, making them more productive and building the bottom line—and around and around it goes, in a constant cycle of change and growth. Change is good for you as a leader and good for your business. Effective leaders don't waste energy fighting inevitable change; they search for opportunities to use that change for the company's advantage.

Change has become essential to the continued growth and development of global business. It stirs things up, cross-fertilizing ideas and aerating the waters of creativity. We may *enjoy* equilibrium, but inactivity soon sours into stagnation. You can't afford complacency, because some hungry young company will always be pushing the envelope and trying to steal part of your market share.

And so it should be: competition makes us stronger, and embracing chaos is good! Corporate leaders sometimes forget this. They let their attitudes and strategies harden in place, assuming what worked well before will always yield success. But, as Harold Geneen, legendary CEO of ITT Corporation, pointed out decades ago: "We must not be hampered by yesterday's myths in concentrating on today's needs."

There was a time not long ago when executives paid lip service to innovation but were the first to block it. For example, Yahoo executives are probably still kicking themselves for turning away the founders of Google, Larry Page and Sergey Brin, when they came looking for investors. Leaders have become much more adept at plugging innovation into their business and corporate cultures; however, some bureaucrats think most new ideas are dangerous, because new ideas can completely change a business when implemented. Often this change proves to be for the better, but naysayers prefer not to chance it—they want to keep doing what has made them successful in the past. The inability to change leads to the slow (or fast) downward spiral of death.

More often than not, the changes passing through our organizations transform them continually, so don't let cultural inertia strangle productivity. You'll inevitably outgrow the old ways of doing things, if only because the technology of business continues to advance at a rapid rate. Your job is to bring order from the chaos and achieve equilibrium from the flux of accelerating change.

IMPLEMENTING SUCCESSFUL INNOVATION

One of the many things Peter Drucker taught us was that only two things actually generate profit: marketing and innovation. Everything else is an expense. Nonetheless, many of us don't want to deal with innovation, because it's too much trouble. New ideas push you out of your comfort zone, requiring you to scramble, to work harder, to think more. For leaders already overstressed by challenging work environments, that's asking a lot.

But we can't just ignore innovation, or we'd all still live in trees and eat bugs. Circumstances force innovation, because it's the only way to avoid stagnation. Innovation provokes changes that must occur for us to move forward. It can be tricky, but there are ways to handle innovation so you can advance your agenda without having the situation blow up in your face. For example:

1 **DON'T TRY TO ACT ON ALL YOUR IDEAS AT ONCE.** Focus on one or two innovations and carry them through to completion. You have only so much time and attention to spare, so pick your best idea and give it your all.

2 **DON'T LET HISTORY HOLD YOU BACK.** If I had a dollar for every time someone told me, "We tried that before, and it didn't work," I could get a nice steak dinner. The thing about change is that it's *change*. Just because something didn't work *before* doesn't mean it won't work *now*. A project that was prohibitively expensive five years ago might be ridiculously cheap today.

3 **DON'T ASSUME THE EXPERTS ARE RIGHT.** Experts once thought humans would never travel faster than thirty-five miles per hour, the speed of a galloping horse.

Nowadays, airplanes regularly exceed five hundred miles per hour. In 1963, Thomas Watson, an IBM executive, stated there would probably never be a market for more than about five computers in the entire world. My family has ten computers in our household alone. One music company exec passed on the Beatles because, as he put it, "Guitar music is on its way out." My point? Even experts sometimes get it wrong. Instead of dismissing an idea because someone's scoffed at it, give it time to grow, then test it to see whether or not anything's there.

Modern companies live and die based on how quickly they can face, embrace, and absorb change. Innovative thinking makes this process easier. But be aware that new ideas *are* risky and when pursued too enthusiastically can slow you down— or they can get shot down because they make people uncomfortable. Yet just because an idea makes someone uncomfortable or hasn't worked in the past doesn't mean you should dismiss it out of hand. No matter how necessary change may be, you'll frequently encounter resistance; after all, it's much easier to stay the same than change. The status quo has inertia on its side.

Overcoming Cultural Inertia

Inertia is simply a tendency to resist change. In physical terms, a body in motion tends to stay in motion in a straight line unless acted upon by an outside force, while a body at rest tends to stay at rest. But the concept of inertia can apply to people, too, and cultural inertia is something you've surely experienced plenty of, even if you didn't have a name for it. You probably know all you care to about bureaucratic inertia, for

example. Once a bureaucracy makes a rule, woe betide those
who try to buck it.

Similarly, some corporate cultures resist change, often to
their detriment, even as the world transforms around them.
Some observers argue that the chief reason Hostess Brands
went bankrupt in 2012 was because it failed to change with
the times, making no attempt to introduce products that ap-
pealed to a more health-conscious demographic.[1] Because they
did nothing, November 16, 2012, became known as The Day
the Twinkie Died.

Facing Down the Juggernaut

In times of plenty, big, slow-moving companies can survive
and even thrive; but when the economy turns upside down,
often they can't find enough resources to keep going. Yet even
the largest company can weather the change-storms if corporate leaders take advantage of—even welcome—the change.

As one of those leaders, how can you divert your organization off a dead-end path?

1 **ENCOURAGE INNOVATION AND INITIATIVE.** "If I wanted
your opinion, I'd ask for it." "I don't pay you to think."
"Stop complaining and get to work." These dinosaur-think-
ing statements should never leave your mouth. Your people
are your greatest resource, and you'll never know what profitable ideas they might come up with if you refuse to listen.
Take advantage of their experience, imagination, and desire
to help; indeed, encourage it.

2 **EMPOWER YOUR TEAM TO OWN THEIR JOBS.** Tell your
people the general direction you want them to go and
let them tell you how to get there. Delegate enough respon-

sibility and authority for your team to do whatever they feel they must without having to ask—and without punishment if something fails. Otherwise, people will keep their heads down to stay out of the line of fire, plodding away, while the go-getters leave to work for someone who appreciates initiative.

3 MAKE YOUR ORGANIZATION WORTH WORKING FOR. Everyone wants to be happy with and proud of their work, yet so few are. Change that. Celebrate the good things. Stop forcing your team members to follow hidebound rules and strategies. Lead by example, exercise scrupulous fairness, and tell your people exactly how their contributions help grow the company. Explain why the goals they reach matter and how each of them can change the world of work.

ADAPTABILITY: LOOKING INTO THE CRYSTAL BALL

When I was growing up, a lot of the items we take for granted now didn't even exist. Those items include cell phones, CDs, email, DVDs, home computers, and satellite radio, to name a few. Now they're commonplace. What will be commonplace ten or twenty-five years from now? There's no telling, but what I *can* say is this: effective business leaders who are ready and willing to embrace the future now will be the ones who prosper for decades to come.

You can succeed in the future only by facing today's challenges head-on, reframing them as opportunities, and taking advantage of them. Stay on top of the trials and tribulations your team will face in the near future. Here are the top five challenges facing today's business leaders:

- *Agile innovation.* Modern business seems unlikely to slow down, thus requiring companies to cultivate an organizational culture of speed, fast decision-making, and quick action. But those can take you only so far if you lack vision.

  Nokia learned this in the 2000s when its leadership decided to forgo smartphone development in favor of "dumb" phones. They had a superb technological team that could have given them a significant head start over everyone else, but they chose to efficiently develop the wrong product. After Apple and others hammered them in the marketplace, they came back with products like the high-end Lumia. Its innovative features and aggressive marketing have taken back a small piece of Nokia's former market share.

- *Competition from emerging nations.* As modern capitalism takes hold in nations that traditionally followed other economic systems or that have begun to become wealthier, we'll see more direct business competition from those countries. According to management consultants McKinsey & Company, by 2025 about 45 percent of the Fortune Global 500 companies will call emerging nations home.[2] Companies that stay on the ball, especially in those emerging markets, will have more opportunities to prosper.

- *Data management.* With the growth of cloud storage and Wi-Fi, data storage has become easier than ever—and data easier to steal. Even traditional data storage methods can fail due to poor management or programming errors. Today, legal regulation of and

penalties for cybertheft vary from country to country.
We lack overriding international laws, much less national
and international task forces, to police crimes of this
nature. Until the law and law enforcement can catch up
with technology, we must take the initiative to protect
and manage our data ourselves.

- *Talent management.* Workers no longer feel a need
  to stay with one company long term, especially if they
  dislike the working conditions. Add in the technological
  revolution, and many workers don't need to go to an
  office on a daily basis. Some have found they don't
  even need traditional leadership. As a leader, you'll
  find yourself becoming more of a facilitator, visionary,
  and cheerleader to tech-savvy, independent-minded
  workers than ever before. Your challenge will be to
  keep finding new ways to encourage your people to
  own their jobs while motivating them to spend their
  discretionary efforts on the organization. You may also
  find that cost-cutting moves you toward less traditional
  workplace solutions, such as increased outsourcing and
  telecommuting for select workers.

- *Focus on adding value.* How you respond to change
  can prove critical during mergers and downsizing.
  Sir Richard Branson, who has overseen hundreds
  of companies, emphasizes the need for tightening
  organizational structure and refusing to take on another
  person's flawed legacy: better to restart the company
  altogether. If you find restructuring necessary, he
  suggests making your organization "very small, very
  specialized, and very expensive."[3]

Star Trek borrowed Shakespeare's phrase "the undiscovered country" to describe the future because we won't recognize it until we see it. But while you lack a map, that doesn't mean you can't hold yourself and your team ready to blaze a trail into that new territory.

With these five challenges in mind, I invite you to move forward and colonize a prosperous new tomorrow, prepared in advance for what's most likely to come. Stay loose, stay agile—and be ready for anything. Striding confidently into the future requires maximizing your preparedness for whatever comes. While perfection may not be possible, there's no reason not to strive for it by continually and incrementally improving your systems, processes, and productivity over time.

Taking Your Team from Good to Superior

If upgrading is so easy, then why do merely good companies still outnumber the superior ones by a factor of hundreds to one? Surely, if the process worked, we'd have seen a flood of great companies by now—and clearly we haven't.

But the problem often isn't the concept—it's the implementation. Leadership frequently fails because we can't see our greatest flaws. It's not simply a matter of not seeing the forest for the trees; we commonly can't see our flaws because we aren't humble enough to accept that a forest exists at all. So I recommended the following four practices:

1 SET ASIDE YOUR EGO. *"Le etat, c'est moi!"* ("The state, it is me!") might have worked for Louis XIV of France, but *you* are not your company, your division, or your team. You lead and represent them, and thus you have an obligation to provide vision and guidance in all things.

So when you make a decision, don't assume that because it

works for you, it works for everyone. For example, a bonus structure awarding you $100,000 if your team reaches certain goals may seem great to you, but it means nothing unless the rest of the team enjoys bonuses as well.

Step up to the plate, lead by example, and take everything and everyone into account before you leap—keeping in mind that the French monarchy ended at the guillotine just a few generations after King Louis XIV made his famous statement.

2 CAREFULLY PICK A DIRECTION AND STICK WITH IT.

You can't become the expert in your field if you don't stay the course long enough. Anyone remember Warner-Lambert? No? It began as a consumer products company with healthcare leanings. From 1979 until 1998, when Pfizer absorbed it, Warner-Lambert completely changed direction at least five times, prompting three major restructurings under three different CEOs. All this did was repeatedly kill its forward momentum, eventually killing the company.

Instead of shifting direction repeatedly, focus on growing what you do best. It's always better to go from being good to being superior at something, rather than spending the same effort to go from abysmal to mediocre to sufficient. Additionally, all team leaders benefit from having a "Not To Do" or "Stop Doing" list—one that states where they shouldn't expend the team's energy and resources.

3 MODEL YOURSELF AFTER THE BEST IN YOUR FIELD.

What can you learn from activities competitors have done right, as well as what they've done wrong? How can you do them one better by using their own methods against them? More than a century ago, the US Postal Service copied many of the business practices of the original Wells Fargo, including the Pony Express and the corner mailboxes still common in some parts of the country. Wells Fargo, after setting the standard, lost the postal game only when government legislation made the USPS the sole legal postal service.

4 **COMMUNICATE INTENTIONALLY.** Effective communication makes a huge difference. Steve Gangwish is a vice president at CSS Farms—a main supplier of potatoes for Frito-Lay, the largest maker of potato chips in the country, and other makers of potato-based products. As Steve pointed out when I talked with him,

> What's made the difference in our team's performance is intentional communication. Every farm has farm meetings once a week, typically on Mondays, and everybody on the farm knows it. Everybody gets together, planning for the week and thinking ahead. It seems that that simple change, toward intentional planning and communication, has made pretty significant impacts in our farms. We've seen where a farm hasn't done this, and as soon as we force them to implement that, all of a sudden they go from low average to above average.

Many other ingredients contribute to the good-to-great recipe, including willingness to work hard, inspiration and innovation, open communication, and encouraging empowerment. I hope these four tips help you break new ground, so you can give your best to anyone who depends on you and your team.

PUTTING FLEXIBILITY INTO ACTION

Inflexible things break, sometimes spectacularly, when stressed. Even metal will come apart if you apply enough strain. So you'll need a flexible approach to survive the business weather. Obviously, the new doesn't *always* work best. Continuous improvement has its flaws if applied to the wrong teams the wrong way, because too-rapid change can stifle ideas before they mature into usefulness. But successful businesses have always adapted readily to change. At no time in living memory—and likely at no point in history—has flexibility been a more desirable business trait than it is today. Change occurs almost daily, whether you want it to or not, so you've got to be able to change course to adapt to new opportunities.

The greatest obstacle to change is usually a reluctance to modify or abandon familiar, comforting procedures. But an agile organization has no choice but to change in the face of reality. Adaptation rules the day. As Nietzsche pointed out, "The snake which cannot cast its skin has to die."

Today's leaders should adopt these six change management methods:

1 EMPLOY ENHANCED FLEXIBILITY. In the change management arena, the need for flexibility is greater than ever. Projects and direction must become ever more flexible; no longer can you try to force them to fit your original specifications and strategies when those become outmoded. Instead of trying to meet requirements that no longer match reality, be open to modifying the scope and direction of projects as you move forward.

2 **AIM FOR CONTROLLED GROWTH.** Enhanced flexibility should occur within a limiting framework, much as the requirements of a sonnet shape and guide poetic creativity. As we move into a business landscape that has been decimated by recent economic troubles, we must take care not to expand too far, too fast. Take time when you need it so you can consolidate your gains. To the extent you have power to do so, you as a leader should carefully choose new directions.

3 **CONSIDER CALCULATED ABANDONMENT.** In the spirit of controlled growth, you may need to help your people adjust to changes that result when company leaders decide to cut losses by selling off or abandoning underperforming projects, markets, or locations. For example, aside from breaking up its Bell Operating Companies by government order in 1982, AT&T has split off whole branches of itself when it has proven expedient to do so—including equipment manufacturing business Lucent Technologies in 1996.

4 **CONSTANTLY UPGRADE YOUR TECHNOLOGY.** Not long ago, typewriters were a staple of office culture. They were displaced in quick succession by word processors, monochrome computers, PCs and Macs, handheld devices, smartphones, and cloud computing . . . all within two dozen years! Every advance toward the paperless office has made work easier, so we can do more of it per unit of time. But you can't become complacent. Just because your team got software upgrades last year doesn't mean they're still cutting-edge; in fact, it might be time to buy new devices to boost their engagement and productivity levels. Given how fast our technology advances, the stuff you were using last year might be given away in cereal boxes next year.

5 **RETUNE YOUR TEAM'S ACTIVITIES REGULARLY.** Stringed
instruments are surprisingly sensitive. By the time you've
finished tuning each string, the first string may be discordant
again. So it goes with work teams, too. While you rarely
want to micromanage, check in with your people regularly to
make sure they're in tune—not only with the team but with
the organization. It's a never-ending process, but if you don't
keep up, you'll end up so far off the beat, you may never find
your way back to the orchestra.

6 **EVOLVE WITH SOCIETY.** No matter how much you
love the product you make or service you provide, it
can become obsolete overnight as society changes. There
aren't many buggy-whip makers anymore. You may have to
change just to stay relevant, so be willing to reconsider your
branding and reinvent yourself occasionally.

Managing Expectations about Change

Project and process management are the meat and potatoes of
the manager's daily work. As an effective leader, you can help
your team become more flexible rather than set in its ways.
How? Try these suggestions:

- Make sure your team understands the *need* for change.
- Communicate the organization's primary goals clearly
  to everyone.
- Find and root out resistance quickly.
- Lead by example.
- Follow by example—i.e., take the path your front-line
  team members recommend, especially regarding strategic
  execution.

- Involve team members in both stating the problem and finding the solution.

- Urge buy-in among senior employees.

- Identify and support the change leaders of the future.

A Bare Beginning

Don't think the pointers I've outlined in this chapter are the *only* things you can do to fight inertia; they're barely a jumping-off point.

You know your team culture best. Just remember: the price of liberty is eternal vigilance—whether you're talking political freedom or corporate freedom of movement. Conscious thought and continual innovation help. Never hesitate to trim organizational fat, drop dying projects, or blow past bureaucracies to get the job done on time and under budget.

If your organization seems to be headed the wrong way, throw your weight against that inertia every way you can. Effective leaders are the best defense against either a corporate charge down the wrong path or a refusal to move at all, but you must be willing to open your eyes to see the future.

Mission

Vision

Cohesion

STRATEGIC THINKING

3
COMMUNICATION

Share Mission,
Vision, and Ideas

Effective communication sets profitable, productive organizations apart from
the duds. It can take many forms, but the
factors that work best are plain talk, honesty,
and cooperation. Your communication must be
simple and straightforward, especially when convey-
ing the organization's mission to employees.

In some cases, particularly when you're working with
other leaders, you also have to know how to butt heads
politely and cautiously. You want to sell your ideas to give an
advantage not only to your team but also to the organization
as a whole.

CONVEYING YOUR MISSION CLEARLY

If you can't effectively communicate the organization's mission and your expectations from the very beginning, you'll
get nowhere. Study the art of getting it right the first time,

which boils down to communicating with the people involved
in whatever project you're working on in the way they best
understand. It's impossible to be either effective or efficient if
your team doesn't understand what they're supposed to be doing in the first place.

Generally, humans like to talk more than they like to listen.
In daily life, this causes enough problems; in the workplace, it
can result in a loss of time and money. Here's an example of a
minor miscommunication that turned into a major issue:

> A technical writer explains to his editor that the client
> wants to use a variant spelling for a specific word on a
> report's cover. Ignoring the request, the editor changes
> that word to the more accepted spelling. The report
> goes to the printer and four hundred copies come back
> perfect-bound. The client rejects the report because of
> the spelling of that *one* word on the cover. The company
> that prepared the report not only has to deal with the
> embarrassment of facing (or losing) the client, but also
> with the unexpected cost of reprinting the documents.

Who deserves the most blame here? The editor—for not lis-
tening. She should have clarified, repeating back to the writer
what she thought she heard him say. *And* the writer—for not
making his point more clearly. He should have followed up
with the editor, in writing as well as verbally, instead of assuming she had listened to and understood his instructions.

Right from the Word "Go"

You can't afford to have your words misinterpreted, lest your
organization suffer. To ensure your team members do their
work correctly the first time, communicate your expectations
clearly and concisely. Follow these three rules:

1 **REPEATEDLY COMMUNICATE YOUR EXPECTATIONS.**
Keep your mission in front of your team. Repeat
your goals until you're blue in the face—you can't
overcommunicate, and you won't insult people with
repetition. You don't always have to communicate your
expectations verbally or in writing; lead by example, too.
If you need your people to work longer hours to meet a
sales quota or push through a rough patch, arrive early and
leave late. Express confidence in their abilities and support
them in every way possible. Modern leaders are visionaries
and facilitators whose lucid vision makes their goals well
known and clear to all.

2 **TRIPLE CHECK FOR UNDERSTANDING.** Rechecking is
especially important when you can't reverse an action,
which is why medical teams that prep surgeries clearly
mark the body part to be removed or operated on. It's also
why demolition crews repeatedly check the address of the
building they're supposed to take down. Sadly, both types
of operations have gone appallingly wrong in the past.
For example, in 2013, one Fort Worth, Texas, demolition
crew demolished the wrong buildings two days in a row.
Apparently, their code enforcement officer failed in both
communications.[4]

3 **COMMUNICATE IN MULTIPLE WAYS.** Keep individual
communication styles in mind. Some people understand
your needs better when you express them verbally; others
do better with written instructions. I recommend using
both. New initiatives deserve team meetings, followed up by
emailed summaries. If you head a larger group, you won't
be able to take everyone's background and capabilities into

account. But even so, make sure your managers know what you need and can communicate it effectively.

At John Hancock Investments, "One of the most important ways we avoid communications breakdowns is through structured communication on a scheduled basis," says Senior Vice President Darren Smith. "These scheduled interactions . . . also lead to greatly increased efficiency, since items of importance can often be grouped together and addressed during scheduled intervals, instead of being a source of constant interruption to all parties."

Trust, but Verify

Effective communication is more art than science, but either way, it requires practice, diligence, and follow-up. Trust your team members to do their jobs, but make sure they understand *what* they should do and *why*. Otherwise, you might demolish the wrong "building" in your organization, and then you'll have some serious explaining to do.

PROMOTING YOUR VISION

Clear communication is important in *all* directions, upward and laterally as well as downward. You'll have to learn to argue effectively and productively with others at or above your responsibility level—because no matter how good-natured people are, if you bring any two together, they'll eventually find something to disagree about.

People who rise to a management level are often competent and strong willed, so you might find yourself at odds with another peer leader or with your own superior. When you're at loggerheads with someone for any reason, you'll want to find the most efficient way to resolve the issue quickly. That way, you can move forward with the business at hand.

I'm not talking about minor opinions that don't matter in the long run. If your team argues about tiny issues, you have bigger problems to work out. No, I mean important issues that can affect your productivity. For example, it could be deciding whether or not to dismiss someone or to submit a negative performance evaluation you disagree with, or how to change a company brand.

Here's how you can argue your point productively, so everyone can move quickly through the dispute phase and get back to work.

1 **GET ALL YOUR DUCKS IN A ROW.** Prepare your arguments, and have your facts straight. Probe them for weaknesses, so you can strengthen your position. Run your thoughts by neutral people and ask them to shoot holes in your argument. You may find your position fails when other factors are brought up, or your view simply has less merit than someone else's. If this proves to be the case, admit your mind has been changed and bow out gracefully.

2 **DISAGREE EARLY, CLEARLY, AND POLITELY.** Remain open to others' points, but make your position clear. Be simple, to the point, and specific about your concerns. If a newly mandated process won't work, explain why, and back your argument up. Once you make others aware of the problem, they can update their requirements to match reality. Don't dispute an argument in general terms; always use specific examples to refute it.

Just as importantly, keep your disagreement clean. Don't use sarcasm or name-calling. Never talk about people behind their backs. These behaviors will rebound on you, solidifying a decision *against* you and damaging team solidarity. Losing your temper can ruin your reputation and hurt your career if the wrong person witnesses or learns of it.

3 **CONSIDER THE OPPOSING ARGUMENT.** Others in a dispute may have several good points, in which case you can integrate those points into your decision-making process and hammer out a compromise. If you don't understand their reasoning, have them explain it to you. They may have an explanation that, when presented logically, will help you understand their position more fully, so then you can give your wholehearted support.

4 **KEEP THE LINES OF COMMUNICATION OPEN.** You can't work something out if you won't talk to one another. Jump on the phone or meet face-to-face instead of sending a volley of email. Present your arguments, listen to the other side, and then decide what to do and how to clear a productive pathway to your goals.

If you've made your argument, but the decision goes against you anyway, grab an oar and start rowing. True leaders can disagree behind closed doors, but when they emerge, they must present a united front. Whether they agreed or not, everyone must accept ownership of a decision in which they participated.

COHESION: FORMING A UNITED FRONT AROUND IDEAS
Sometimes head-butting results from your attempts to promote a new idea, strategy, or beneficial expenditure. In this type of case, you have to tune up your effective persuasion skills to sell the idea, which requires a different approach to disagreement.

From Paper to Reality

Every innovation—from the fishhook to the Space Shuttle—started with an intangible idea. In business, new ideas help us improve everything from work processes to our product lines. We depend on innovation to survive. But innovation won't get you *anywhere* if you can't communicate it widely.

Those who operate businesses aren't always open to new ideas. As we discussed in chapter 2, they may prefer to stick with what they know, rather than take a chance on something unproven. There may come a time when one of your team's carefully nurtured ideas has matured into something truly useful. Now you just have to get it past the defenses of the people whose failure to support it may result in its death. Depending on the organization, those people may consider dozens of ideas a month, or rarely hear any at all. Either way, they can stymie your initiative, so know the answer to this question: what makes your idea different enough to be heard?

Cautionary Tales

You don't hear much about the ideas upper management shoots down. When no one cares enough for an idea to fight for it successfully, that may be a sign it's either flawed or ahead of its time. But there are also lots of examples of ideas whose time *had* come, but that stalled (at least temporarily) because of bad judgment. Take Western Union's decision not to buy the patent for the telephone in 1876, citing it as an "electric toy." That toy spawned an entire trillion-dollar business.

To keep your big idea from getting the brush-off, start by outlining the implementation process ahead of time. When I was on the board of directors for the National Speakers Association, certain board members had a habit of asking about the implementation plan *before* approving a proposal. Imagine that! They wanted to know an idea's originators had thought through the next steps and were ready to spring into action. The board wasn't impressed with half-baked ideas and hazy answers—they wanted to know proposers knew what they were doing.

Then do your homework, so you can answer any question a skeptical manager or board member may ask. How will your idea impact the organization? How much will it earn the company, above and beyond its cost?

To be sure you've worked out all the angles, pitch your idea to a trusted but critical colleague first and ask that person to tear holes in it. If the holes can't be fixed, drop it. Then, when you do pitch the idea, reveal the win right away. Don't bury your conclusions in a mountain of data or glib assurances. Start with your most important point: why and how this idea can profit the organization. Once you have your audience's attention, *then* you can outline the details and explain how you plan to implement it.

You can take a page from the marketing department's playbook while preparing for this process, using these two important strategies:

First, address the objections. Any good salesperson will tell you that to sell something, you have to be able to address all the objections the buyer has. List every objection you might expect someone to make, prepare detailed rebuttals, and memorize them. When the objections arise, you've either sent answers in advance in an FAQ sheet, or you'll be able to address concerns to everyone's satisfaction.

Second, list the benefits. Once you've dealt with the objections, show everyone why your idea profits them in particular and the organization in general. List the benefits in descending order of importance, vividly illustrate their value, and show they're obtainable with a modicum of effort.

World Changers

One idea can change the world. Planes, trains, and automobiles are all good examples. At the very least, your idea can change your organization. But it won't go anywhere unless you know how to present it to those in power—and fight for it through the worst of their criticism.

Your idea may not make it, but who knows? You may end up the world's next Sergey Brin or Steve Jobs. Don't give up on an idea until it's truly dead. Even then, you may be able to resurrect it later as technology and society advance.

Resolve

Collaborate

Execute

STRATEGIC
THINKING

4

DECISION-MAKING

Resolve and Execute
Decisions Promptly

Motion beats meditation—once you've contemplated the situation enough to know what actions to take. Too often, indecision rules in the workplace, because decision-makers fear making mistakes. Yet the occasional mistake is the price of effective decision-making. It's better to take a wrong turn than no turn at all. You can always change direction to correct an error or to meet a new threat or opportunity head-on. Dithering is neither effective nor efficient, and a successful business leader will avoid it.

In addition to making decisions that push you ahead, you have to decide to fix what's already wrong in your team or organization. Don't fall for the belief that disagreement within the team is something you should squelch. Friction can be positive, as long as it lets you see all sides of the story before you make the final decision.

Once you've made a decision, *act on it*. In business, the only thing that really matters is results. You don't get results until you execute, so trade theory for action and get moving. When you've got a rough plan of action in place, move from meditation to motion—and stay in motion until you're done.

RESOLVE INDECISION

Procrastination. Perfectionism. Waiting for more information. Fear in all its forms. There are dozens of reasons—maybe hundreds—for staying safely within your comfort zone rather than stepping out into the dangerous, prickly world of change. Some may even seem logical. After all, you will face change whether you like it or not, so why deliberately add even more to the agenda?

Well, there's the old "stagnation is death" argument: If you don't change, you can't grow. But maybe you don't care about growing, only surviving. If so, answer this question: is spending a career fighting rearguard actions as everyone else tries to run over you worth all the effort? Wouldn't life be easier if you were pushing forward—or even better, running at the front of the pack, completely in the clear?

The Curse of Caution

Even ambitious people have a tendency to overthink things. But thinking for too long quickly hits a point of diminishing returns. In the words of philosopher Ralph Waldo Emerson, "An ounce of action is worth a ton of theory."

There's an image making the rounds on the Internet titled "Executive Decision Making System." It shows both faces of a penny, with heads labeled "Yes" and tails labeled "No." There have probably been times when you wish you could just flip a coin to settle something, rather than wading through the pros and cons. But don't you feel better after having made a decision? Most of us do.

Instead of digging in your pocket for that coin and letting fate make the decision for you, test your choices against these imperatives:

- *Core values, mission, and vision.* If you're in alignment with your organization's core values, some decisions will come surprisingly easily. Ditto for mission and vision.

- *Outcome.* Follow the decision to its logical conclusion. Can you see danger lurking somewhere down that path? Is this a slippery-slope choice that could lead to other bad decisions? Does one possible outcome satisfy you more than the others? What contingency plans can you put into place?

- *Return on investment (ROI).* This is crucial for most businesses. Will your decision make your company more money than it spends? Include all the factors you can think of, and remember: it's what happens in the long run that counts. Saving money this month by laying off a third of your workforce won't help you long term if the rest keel over from exhaustion or leave in droves, causing your company to fall apart.

- *Opportunity cost.* Every choice you make closes other doors. If you decide to do something, what will it keep you from doing in the future? Is what you skip worth missing out on? What other trade-offs will you face?

- *Efficient use of time and resources.* Will this decision slow workflow and efficiency in your organization? If so, you'd better choose "tails," unless some other benefit offsets the wasted resources.

Make Up Your Mind, Already!

You make a decision even when you refuse to act, but that's no better than depending on a coin toss. Don't simply *react* to the world as it changes; be *proactive* about changing it. Give all your business decisions careful consideration before you make them, but don't let meditation overcome motion. And never *ever* let chance dictate your organization's fate because you failed to make a decision.

But What If You're Wrong?

This question plagues all decision-makers, from rank amateurs to seasoned veterans. If you're wrong, so be it. A wrong decision usually won't decide the fate of your organization or even an individual. Even if it does, at least you didn't sit around and do nothing. You tried.

You probably know the consequences of analysis paralysis. "Vapor-lock" of the brain can kill a project through indecision as surely as pulling its funding would. In fact, pulling the funding is cleaner. Then the project dies suddenly, rather than flopping around like a fish out of water and damaging the whole team or company.

Cases in point: video game company 3D Realms wasted twelve years and tens of millions of dollars on the sequel to their popular game Duke Nukem 3D before abandoning the effort.[5] Similarly, LucasArts, a legendary gaming company that failed in April 2013, collapsed because of indecision and apathy at the highest levels.[6] Somehow, the creators of *Star Wars* and Indiana Jones couldn't be bothered to make any new games after having taken the industry by storm with these inventive new entries in the mid- to late 1980s.

Buckling Down

So what should you do when faced with an uncertain decision? Follow these tips so you're covered as best you can be:

1 CONSIDER AS MANY OPTIONS AS POSSIBLE WITHOUT STALLING. Don't leap before you look, but don't spend forever looking, either. Moving quickly doesn't mean making a knee-jerk decision. Gather relevant facts, ignore your ego, listen to advisers, consider the repercussions—then make the best move for your organization and team.

2 TAKE REASONABLE PRECAUTIONS. Hedge your bets before making your decision, just in case something unexpected happens. Even if you're excited about a prospect, that's no reason to forget about due diligence. A classic example: Time Warner's acquisition of AOL in 2000. Time Warner Chairman Gerald Levin was so eager to make the deal that he didn't put a standard contingency plan in place to back out or revisit the terms of the deal if AOL's stock underperformed. AOL was vastly overvalued, so when the dot-com bubble burst and AOL's stock dropped 50 percent overnight, Time Warner found itself $200 billion in the hole.[7]

3 DON'T HESITATE TO REVERSE DIRECTION. It makes no sense to keep digging a hole when you've obviously made the wrong decision. Abandoning a bad decision gives you room to make a better one. Back up, look over the situation, and try a different tack once you have enough information to proceed.

4 **DON'T AUTOMATICALLY DISMISS NEW OPPORTUNITIES.**
Even if it seems too good to be true, investigate any intriguing opportunity to profit—and think twice about not pursuing it, no matter how logical your reasoning. For example, Kodak invented the digital camera in 1975, then suppressed its existence because the company didn't want digital options to hurt its film sales.[8] Later, it could have been named the official film of the 1984 Olympics, but gave up the opportunity to a brash new competitor, Fuji.[9] At the time, Kodak controlled 90 percent of the photographic film market. In 2012, it went into Chapter 11.[10]

Take Charge

If you're in command, be in command. Your superiors put you where you are so you could move your company forward. The only way to move forward? Make decisions. Lots of them. Constantly. If you make five wrong decisions, you've ruled out five things that won't work. Remain flexible, and always be willing to try a new direction when something fails.

COLLABORATE AROUND DECISION-MAKING

You have a staff for a reason—to handle the pressure of everyday operations. Then you can handle the important things, including decisions that determine your team's or organization's direction. You can even have your people contribute their ideas and prove, by doing, what works and what doesn't.

Sometimes this collaborative approach can result in workplace conflict. But friction isn't always a bad thing, especially when you leverage it by giving everyone a voice in decision-making through healthy debate. This strengthens the team, allows constructive change, and short-circuits problems.

Healthy Disagreement

Many leaders consider conflict between employees to be a dangerous thing, and no wonder. No doubt you've seen the productivity-killing results of clashing personalities and company politics. Some managers go to great lengths to avoid conflict, but overcompensation devolves into complacency or, worse, groupthink—where everyone thinks alike and disagreement can't be tolerated. "Yes men" have doomed more than one company.

Consider Blackberry. Once the fastest-growing company in the world, it has recently faded into near-obscurity. Rather than face the reality that consumer rather than business applications would drive smartphone sales, Blackberry execs turned their backs on consumers—and lost their market share to iPhones and Android devices.[11] Maybe a little dissension in the ranks would have done some good.

At flooring provider Shaw Industries, healthy debate is a normal part of the decision-making process. As Vice President of Marketing Brenda Knowles said in a recent interview,

> We value diversity of backgrounds and thought, and seek that when putting together teams. That naturally brings with it differing opinions on how to approach something or what the root of any particular challenge may be. But that's what we want. That deep respect for your colleagues

invites healthy debate that will get us to the best answer. We aim to foster a culture of candor that is respectful yet provocative. We believe that healthy debate, or healthy conflict as we often reference it, has been a big part of our business success.

The Flip Side of Conflict

Conflict doesn't have to stifle innovation or bring your work-flow to a screeching halt. Dissension has its place within work-place discussions. If nothing else, it lets people blow off steam and feel more engaged—crucial factors in performance and productivity. Better yet, you may hear some innovative ideas with the potential to revitalize your business or fatten the bottom line.

Let's look at the reasons to let team members clash at times:

- *Conflict sparks healthy debate and competition.* When people can argue about where they're going, you avoid the blind agreement that characterizes groupthink. It also stirs up the team culture, especially when handled in a professional manner. If an idea looks like it won't work, let debate sort it out—don't just cut it down immediately. Some ideas need time to mature.

- *Conflict gives everyone a voice in decision-making,* making sure no one feels left out, thereby enhancing commitment and engagement. That's an integral part of the CSS Farms management process, according to Vice President Steve Gangwish. "When people come to work in the morning and go home at night, they feel like it's their deal, their farm."

Giving everyone a voice also results in a better understanding of one's teammates. When you air your differences, you learn why others think the way they do—and this might change your own mind. At the very least, the discussion provides new insight into another person's approach and beliefs, even if you continue to disagree.

• *Conflict allows constructive change.*
Well-reasoned disagreement, especially when the dissenter stands by it, can result in improvement not only for one project but for subsequent ones as well. Have you ever seen the film *12 Angry Men*, or read the play it's based on? If one juror hadn't stood by his beliefs and disproved the "evidence," an innocent man might have been convicted. In challenging the status quo, the juror shattered long-held assumptions and personal agendas.

• *Conflict short-circuits worse problems.*
Rather than letting resentment fester into something truly dangerous, properly handled conflict allows individuals to resolve their differences before they explode.

A Delicate Equilibrium
When you work through conflict instead of suppressing or ignoring it, it strengthens the team—and a stronger team is more productive. Colorless groupthink serves you poorly in business, so within specific guidelines, allow your people some level of conflict. Careful handling of honest disagreements can inject a much-needed breath of fresh air into the workplace atmosphere.

EXECUTE DECISIONS AND MOVE FORWARD

Once you've made the decision, execute! When it comes to productivity and success, execution trumps all. No matter how well you've planned your strategy, nothing happens if you don't get it done.

If your people are dragging their feet, shake them up a bit. As a leader, it's your responsibility to elicit results. Depending on your style and your generation, you may interpret that to mean directly facilitating team progress without making friends—fast becoming an antiquated viewpoint—or chilling with your people over a beer every once in a while. In either scenario, the ability to make ideas happen means the difference between success and failure, so sometimes you have to set a hard line and be the boss. That means, among other things:

1 **STOP ACCEPTING EXCUSES.** If lack of training or equipment slows productivity, rectify the situation. If people still don't produce, find out why and correct the issues in whatever way necessary.

2 **SET STRICT DEADLINES.** Make team goals clear, while setting drop-dead dates for producing what you and your superiors require. If necessary, create an action plan mapping the major deadlines along the way. Outline exactly how you'll go about reaching those milestones, and then choose the clearest path that lets you leap straight into action.

3 **DON'T OVERCOMPLICATE.** All you need is a basic roadmap, so choose the easiest, cheapest way to execute the mission. Embrace flexibility so you can turn on a dime if the situation warrants. Avoid making success contingent

on a particular step or item, or you may end up dead in the water; always leave room for a workaround.

4 **HONE THEIR SKILLS.** When it doesn't interfere with productivity, send your team to training, even for skills they might not need right now but will in the future. Urge them to invest in continuing education to increase their personal ROIs. Many organizations will pay for it as long as employees maintain their quality of work.

5 **HELP THEM STRUCTURE THEIR TIME.** If a team member can't get it together, intervene a bit more than usual on the scheduling. You can have low performers submit personal schedules for your approval and require activity reports if you can't see results. If those steps don't work, put them on a corrective action plan.

Get a Move On

Know this: you'll never get as much information as you'd like before you start on a project. You'll never be able to account for every contingency and detail. You'll feel nervous when you make a decision, especially when you embark on something new. But don't let any of that—or fear or procrastination or any other excuse—keep your team from moving forward. Other people depend on you to make a final decision, so they can move forward.

Taking action overcomes fear—and ideas are worthless until you take action. So once you have enough ducks in a row, get started and meet the challenge head-on. You can take care of the details as they arise. Stop dragging your heels and get to it, selecting the easiest, most direct path to success—exercising simplicity, careful direction, practicality, speed, and flexibility along the way.

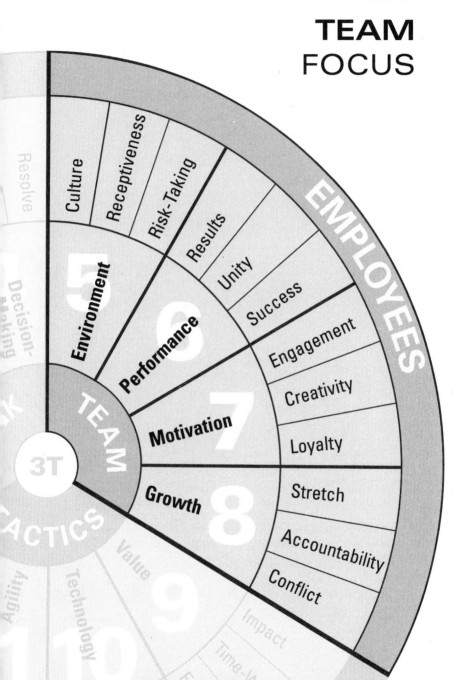

Effective, efficient executives take responsibility for the return on investment (ROI) their teams generate, because doing so benefits the entire organization. Getting discretionary effort from team members begins with a genuine concern for them and their lives—an approach that previous generations of executives might have found a little too touchy-feely for their liking. Some still do. But during the past generation or so, something unusual has happened: executives have evolved from being bosses to being team members. Oh, they're still in charge, but smart leaders realize they get further by forming partnerships with their employees.

Modern executives act mostly as visionary facilitators, even cheerleaders, rather than as dictators. They drive strategy with team input as part of their leadership role and encourage team members to deploy their own tactics for achieving goals. Why? By necessity.

Strategy is more fluid and responsive to change than ever before, so everyone has to execute in whatever way works best at a particular moment. Since the Great Recession hit in 2008, managerial and individual contributor roles have started converging. No longer can leaders consider themselves completely distinct from nonmanagerial teammates. Business has always been a collaborative endeavor, and today it must become even more so to facilitate efficient execution and greater productivity.

EXECUTIVE IMPROVEMENT 101

You depend on your team at least as much as they depend on you—probably more. So before we get into how to maintain a team focus in the next four chapters, let's consider some principles first:

1 SINCERELY VIEW EMPLOYEES AS YOUR GREATEST ASSET. Everyone *says* they do this, but in our precarious economy, some leaders still see employees as replaceable. True, they must be to some extent, since no one— even you—should be indispensable. People must be able to be promoted, and the company must survive without key people if they die, fall ill, or leave. But employees are not interchangeable machine parts. They're people. If you take care of them, they're more likely to take care of you— loyalty cuts both ways.

In a knowledge-based economy, your teammates become especially valuable, because their skills are completely portable; they live in those few pounds of gray matter between their ears. Treat them well so they'll stay with you—good workers cost a lot to replace.

Care for your team, too. Don't act like a distant emi-
nence more worried about your annual bonus than your
people. It's easier for your team to like you if you care
about them, so make it obvious you do. If your people
are happier, they'll perform better, and you'll all prosper
as a result.

2 COMMUNICATE LEADERSHIP BY WORD AND DEED.
Talk is cheap. If you can't keep a promise, don't make
it. Otherwise, ask your people what would increase their job
satisfaction and performance—and then pursue putting those
factors in place.

Promises are important, particularly where goals are
concerned. Similarly, don't demand the kind of hard work
and focus you won't do yourself. You'll have your team's
loyalty if you're in there actively working with them, insofar
as your duties allow. You won't garner respect if you roll
in at 10 A.M. and leave at 4 P.M. to play golf during a tough
time, even if you're on the course schmoozing to capture
a new account.

Darren Smith, Senior Vice President at John Hancock
Investments, encourages continuous improvement by ex-
pecting it in himself. "If a company and its leaders are always trying to push forward and get just a little better every
day, to reach a little higher every day, and to make more of
a difference every day, it quickly filters down through the
company," he points out. "It's also critical to equip team
members with the ability to define and measure improvement, and also recognize when there's a lack of progress
toward the stated objectives."

3 UNLOCK THEIR ENTHUSIASM AND ENERGY.

Find reasons for your team members to pour their discretionary effort into their work. Empower them in every way possible, share your authority, and provide top incentives in whatever forms work best. Given the need to do your own work, remain as accessible as you can and don't micromanage. Instead, trust your folks to do what they need to do and make it easier for them to do it. Tackle your own work with enthusiasm and verve.

Allowing your people to do their jobs without too much interference can work wonders. Steve Gangwish of CSS Farms points to autonomy as a big part of the loyalty recipe in his company. "We rely on leaders to be autonomous and manage their operations on their own. While we have weekly communications with everybody, a corporate leader may only get to their site a couple of times a year. So the other three hundred sixty days of the year, [the farm managers] are in charge."

4 PROVIDE TRAINING. Give your employees the

intellectual and educational tools they need to maximize their potential. Teach them to ask themselves, "Did I pay for myself today?" If the answer is no, they may need more training. Give it to them so everyone can benefit. Make the option available to everyone who qualifies and allow them as much room to improve as they can handle. You'll more than earn back the cost in increased productivity and goodwill. For example, I've recovered the investment made in my virtual admin's WordPress training by huge margins.

What matters in the end is ROI, not initial cost. If you can make more money by improving your employees' performance than you spend on doing so, then do it. When employees specifically tell you how you can help them boost their productivity, listen up!

Better in Every Way

If you keep these points in mind and take care to implement the suggestions outlined in the next four chapters, you'll inevitably improve your team's performance. And you may just improve the whole company's well-being along the way.

REMEMBER

Keep this central thesis in mind: Never lose track of your team's best interests while pursuing your own. That's one touchstone of a good executive.

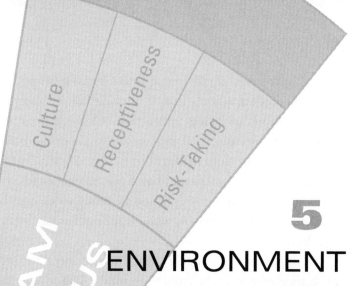

Culture

Receptiveness

Risk-Taking

TEAM FOCUS

5
ENVIRONMENT

Build an
Open Team Culture

In a business sense, a "culture" is the social setting in which work takes place. Sometimes it forms spontaneously, evolving out of a set of core values and combining with corporate mission, vision, and basic goals. "Culture" can also be an unwritten set of mutually understood rules, such as "We typically start meetings five minutes late around here." The efficient, effective executive takes a direct hand in guiding organizational culture, while making a deliberate effort to maintain a positive culture where it already exists.

Work culture in general has recently moved toward increased agility, flexibility, and speed, punctuated by periods of rapid evolution. To get ahead, you can't fear change. Learn to quickly bounce back when something doesn't work the way you intend.

Calculated risk is still an important basis of corporate culture, but leaders can no longer calculate all the variables for months before springing into action. Overcollaboration and overcautious decision-making takes more time than businesses can afford. Move from meditation to motion as quickly as possible, making instant changes based on the challenges you run into. You must move swiftly and be ready to change course on the spur of the moment, while realizing that flexibility rules the day.

It's important to recognize that you may need to force the evolution of corporate culture at times. This occurs by aggressively adopting new technologies and strategies, as well as emphasizing force multipliers such as delegation, accountability, and communication. You also have to challenge your best people to become even better.

Most of how your team culture develops boils down to what you do as a leader. The easier you make it for your team to excel, the more likely they will. So get on your managerial bulldozer and remove the obstacles to your team's success. Encourage teamwork, empower everyone, and emphasize accountability. Root out any internal limitations.

An effective, efficient executive must also be willing to fight in his or her corner, protecting the team in every way possible. You may have to rock the boat to get what you and your people need, which sometimes means making a sacrifice for the team.

CREATING A CULTURE OF TEAM EFFICIENCY

Business is becoming more complicated, competitive, and unpredictable by the day. Those in leadership positions must be constantly aware of this reality, because the decisions made affect the lives and careers of everyone on the team, and sometimes influence the fate of the entire organization.

Every once in a while, you have to stop, take a good look around, and breathe deeply—and then do whatever it takes to reduce the outrageous complexity everyone faces.

Bitter Truths

Organizations often grow top-heavy because leaders won't let go of old responsibilities when they take on new ones—even when the old ones are money pits. Analysts Simon Collinson and Melvin Jay, writing in *The European Business Review* in 2011, estimated that the two hundred largest Fortune 500 companies alone suffer from "value-destructive complexity," costing them $237 billion a year.[12]

Aside from an unwillingness to abandon unworkable initiatives, leaders create unnecessary complexity when they:

- Overthink business situations.
- Overengineer products and services.
- Lose focus on what truly matters.
- Avoid handling important issues.
- Repeatedly reinvent the process "wheel."
- Aimlessly chase unclear goals.
- Fear that simplifying means eliminating jobs.

Instead of crashing and burning against the wall of over-complexity, hit the brakes, take your sledgehammer out of the trunk, and start breaking down the wall so you can move forward. Here's the hammer—four tools you can use to simplify your life:

1 STREAMLINE WORKFLOW PROCESSES.
Constantly tweak your workflow by:

- Trying new things.
- Clearing your team's path.

- Slashing bureaucracy.
- Replacing broken and underperforming "parts."
- Occasionally overhauling the whole work engine if necessary.

This requires a persistent situational awareness of your team's productivity from moment to moment, combined with a willingness to step forward and make relevant changes if your people don't do so on their own. As a leader, you're responsible for making things easier and faster for your team.

2 **APPLY SIMPLE RULES TO BUSINESS SITUATIONS.** Don't build elaborate decision-making and process flow frameworks. This goes double for your most complex issues. Cut items that don't fit organizational objectives. If an initiative or endeavor fails to move the company forward, cut it loose and move on. Quickly identify process bottlenecks, create a few simple guidelines for handling them, and put those guidelines into action. You may discover that rather than having dozens of processes to deal with, you actually have one core process that applies to dozens of situations. Cleaning up your processes accelerates business wonderfully, resulting in greater simplicity *and* greater profits.

3 **CUT UNNECESSARY POSITIONS.** Simplifying may mean you no longer need as many people to do the job as you once did. While no one likes to let people go, restructuring may be necessary for the organization's survival. After all, if the company fails, everyone loses. However, it's always better to decrease head count through transfers, attrition, retirement, and lateral promotions first.

4 INCLUDE A SUNSET CLAUSE FOR ALL PROJECTS AND INITIATIVES.

Make the end of an endeavor part of its natural life cycle. Plan for that ending, and when it comes time to shut down, do so—unless there's an overriding reason to continue.

You can demonstrate your commitment to efficiency by actively working to simplify business processes with your team and working to get buy-in from other leaders as well.

Calculated Reduction

In my 2012 book *What to Do When There's Too Much to Do,* I introduced the mantra of "reduce, reduce, reduce." This works as well with excess complexity as it does with most aspects of business.

Keep this in the forefront of your mind, because it's human nature to overcomplicate situations; we all want a hand in the solution, and no one wants to tell anyone else no. You have a choice: you can build tottering towers of business complexity doomed to eventual failure, or you can pare them down to stable, simple structures that will stand indefinitely.

INCREASING TEAM RECEPTIVENESS TOWARD SWIFT EXECUTION

Change already moves at a breakneck pace in the business world. Three- to five-year strategic plans no longer work, since they go stale within months. These words from my client Mike Howard, Chief Security Officer of Microsoft, leap to mind: "Remember: strategy is not like the Ten Commandments. It's not written in stone. It depends on the circumstances—which could include anything from budget changes to a change in leadership or a change in world events."

Front-line employees need the permission and the flexibility to work with any tactics available to them to execute in the moment—to do what's required to achieve company goals. Therefore, you have no choice except to make your business move faster, without sacrificing quality. Implement these techniques in your quest for speed:

1 **MONITOR TRENDS WITHIN YOUR INDUSTRY.** Know what's coming over the horizon and what's nipping at your heels, so you can stay ahead of the pack. If Borders Books and Music —a personal favorite of mine that failed back in 2011—had responded more quickly and appropriately to far-reaching changes in the publishing industry, it might still exist.[13]

2 **REWARD EFFICIENCY.** If someone on your team comes up with an efficient way to save time or enhance workflow, reward that person with a bonus, a raise, more vacation time, or whatever seems appropriate.

3 **TAKE ADVANTAGE OF OPPORTUNITIES AS THEY ARISE.** If you have limited time to grab hold of something that can benefit you and your team, don't dawdle. Either do it or don't. Don't take a year to implement a decision; have a sense of urgency.

Need for Speed

You don't have to be superhuman to succeed in business; you just need to tank up with high-octane fuel. Tips like these will help you bypass competitors who haven't yet realized the need for speed. Nowadays, consumers want instant gratification. If you don't give it to them, they'll find someone who will.

Innovate Constantly

If I had to pick only one piece of business advice that's become pure cliché over the past few decades, I'd pick "think outside the box." Because it's so overused, I have to resist rolling my eyes when I hear it. But the lesson remains valid: don't let your preconceptions, habits, or narrow-mindedness keep you from considering all parts of a problem. Outgrow your mental constraints and consider all the information at your disposal.

I hate to pick on Borders, but I still miss them years after they went out of business. They offered a nice alternative to the other "big-box" retailers, with a wide selection and wonderful customer service.

But the company's failure to acknowledge that electronic publishing really *did* represent the wave of the future helped kill them. Their executives couldn't see beyond their own boundaries. In addition, they overextended financially.[14] Sadly, it became clear something was wrong more than a year before Borders declared bankruptcy. For example, I went into their stores and noticed every other light was turned off, and customer service wasn't as responsive as usual. They'd even put out computers to let people look up and order books on their own. While that was a nice touch, when a company has to scrimp on its energy bills and customer service to survive, it's already seen the writing on the wall.

The Barnes and Noble chain, on the other hand, survives partly because it developed its own electronic publishing branch, complete with an exclusive e-reader, the Nook. Nook started off with attractive color models in 2009.[15] Compare that with Amazon's Kindle, which didn't release color models until 2011.[16]

Exiting the Proverbial Box

Taking full advantage of all your resources, both your own and those of your colleagues and teammates, blasts the lid off the "box." Just make sure that while doing so, you don't create another box—or step so far outside your comfort zone you have no idea where to go from there. Reinforce these five concepts with your team:

1 **MONITOR NEW TECHNOLOGY.** Even when you think it doesn't affect you, study technological advances and how they impact other industries. You may find a way to turn them to your advantage. Consider Starbucks. Do you think of it as *just* a place to get a cup of joe? Of course not. They've successfully integrated product placement from other industries, especially music; they offer travel mugs, a wide variety of ground and whole bean coffees, and other similar ancillary products. They even offer food now. More to the point, they've made themselves the go-to place for people who want to casually read in a comfortable environment, work on their computers, or simply tap into free Wi-Fi.

2 **NEVER STOP LOOKING FOR NEW IDEAS.** The McDonald's restaurant chain has enormous innovation skills. It began when the original McDonald brothers applied assembly-line methods to fast food production. This continued when Ray Kroc bought the company and started franchising the methodology.

3 **ENCOURAGE DIVERSITY.** You'll have to fill certain work slots with whomever fits best, but typically, the greater the variety of people you have on your staff, the more likely you'll survive tough times and boost innovation. Diversity in work experience, culture, personality, scholastic background, and even age can help your team survive when others do not.

4 PUSH YOUR BOUNDARIES. Even if you never completely leave your box (you have to specialize in *something*), constantly push against its walls and redefine its limits. If nothing else, this teaches you what works and what doesn't. Nike, Inc. has done this over the years, producing hundreds of different styles of shoes for every kind of foot and activity. Nike also created the "Just Do It" advertising slogan, which simply and directly inspires people to push the envelope.

5 START SMALL. Smart leaders start with baby steps to make sure their core market approves changes. When the Gerber baby food company tried to sell adult entrees in the 1970s, they hit stiff resistance . . . and wisely gave up on the idea. Luckily, they hadn't overinvested in the venture, and it didn't take long before they went back to making baby food full time.[17] Sometimes diversifying just doesn't work when it steps too far beyond your usual product line.

Throwing Away the Box Altogether

Silly Putty[18] and the Slinky[19] are classic kids' toys that emerged from attempts during World War II to create an artificial rubber and a kind of shock absorber for sensitive naval instruments, respectively. Neither product worked for the task it was originally intended for, but each did have remarkable properties. If the inventors had failed to think outside their narrow wartime boxes, nothing would have become of either invention. Instead, those inventors opened their minds to all the possibilities and made millions because of it.

CHALLENGE YOUR TEAM
AND REWARD RISK-TAKING

As you build and refine team culture, you'll consistently have trouble challenging your best and brightest enough to keep them engaged with their work. While we're all created equal, that doesn't mean we're all the *same*. When bright people combine their intelligence with drive and hard work, they can achieve much more than average employees.

Good news. You undoubtedly have bright people working for you, which can result in higher team productivity. But the situation does come with its drawbacks, as bright people tend to get bored easily . . . and, as in school, bored smart kids often act out. The solution? Challenge them!

The Right Motivation

Forget offering bored employees the same old "brass rings" to grab for. Make them want to go for the gold. By "gold," I don't necessarily mean financial motivation, though that may help. What they *really* need is purpose: a chance to excel at something that matters. Workers who focus on completing specific tasks consistently, or on helping those in need, tend to have lower "boreout" levels.[20] This intervention works best when you learn how to recognize when bored workers are pretending to be busy so they won't be found out and let go. Once you pierce that camouflage, give those workers the opportunity to prove they can excel. Here's how:

1 KEEP THE COMMUNICATION LINES OPEN. Touch base regularly with your top employees, allowing them open access to you. Stay alert for signs of boredom. Ask them what they're working on that excites them—or what *would* excite them if nothing currently does.

2 **OFFER THEM TASKS WITH A REAL CHANCE OF FAILURE.**
This may sound like odd advice, but you likely have
blue-sky projects that could be extremely profitable if done
well. They're challenging enough that most people can't
achieve success, so hand these to your bright but bored. The
intellectual challenge will help them channel their boredom—and any risk-taking behavior associated with it—into
potential success. If there's no possibility of failure, then
where's the thrill when they succeed?

3 **KEEP THEM BUSY.** Pile your employees' plates full of
a variety of tasks, so when one gets boring, they can
jump to another. Keep those plates full until they cry uncle,
and then help them prioritize. All your team's tasks should
produce results worthy of their talents; busywork does
nothing for the team's bottom line. And don't worry about
overworking superstars. When Sirota Consulting conducted
a study of 800,000 employees at sixty-one organizations in
2009, they found that workers with too little work posted
an average job satisfaction rating of 49 percent—while those
with too *much* work reported a job satisfaction rating of 57
percent.[21] Don't forget, the operative word here is *challenge*.

4 **HELP THEM FALL IN LOVE WITH THE PROCESS.** Anyone
can work hard when motivated. But in real life, consistent productivity means bulling one's way through the
dull patches, producing even when doing less-than-inspiring
work. If you can help your bored employees fall in love
with the *process* of marketing, coding, writing, speaking, or
whatever their job entails, they'll never be bored. They'll
always have something to anticipate or polish. Also, find
ways to help them embrace the boredom that naturally

comes with any job. How? Teach them to anticipate the reward that comes *after* the humdrum—that is, a sense of accomplishment.

Stepping It Up

Employee boredom can corrode morale and productivity not only for those who are bored but also for those to whom they complain. There's no reason to allow complaining when you can step up and actively fight it. You may not eliminate boredom altogether among your brighter employees, but, if you keep an eye on the situation and implement the simple tips to motivate them, you can definitely fight it to a draw.

Fight for Your Slice of the Pie

Given today's global market and the exploding Chinese and Indian economies, business has become more competitive than ever. In years to come, many more Fortune 500 companies will be headquartered in developing countries.[22] While that provides more opportunity, because the pie has grown bigger, companies still have to scramble for their slices.

Similarly, with limited internal resources in any company, if you don't fight for your team, you may find yourself dealing with scarce resources just when you need them most.

Put Your Team First

No doubt you've seen too many self-serving maneuvers over the years to be surprised when a leader slinks off into everyone-for-himself-or-herself territory. So why not surprise your team by facing your in-house rivals like a team player? Keep these three tips in mind when the going gets tough:

1 **PRESENT YOUR NEEDS CLEARLY.** Who gets the resources he or she needs: the shrinking violet or the fighter who asks for them? Too often, I've seen people curse the darkness when they could just flip the light switch. If you don't get what you want, ask for it. See your superior(s) and outline your needs, especially if you've just landed something new and urgent. Don't make demands, but don't shy away from your duty to provide for your team, either. They can't proceed unless you provide for them.

At the same time, make sure those you compete with for resources know it isn't personal—you're still a team player, and you're trying to build the company by building your team. Keep adding value in every way possible.

2 **STAND UP FOR YOUR TEAM.** Whether they've gotten in trouble for doing something controversial or the company is reducing head count, defend your people. Your team needs to know you're on their side, come what may. This is especially true when someone tries to poach team members or lay them off. Each person who leaves changes the team dynamic and can reduce productivity—unless the departing team member was a poor performer or saboteur.

3 **TAKE ONE FOR THE TEAM.** Nobody wants to suffer when troubles come along—but to protect your team, you may have to. If you head a large division and your CEO orders you to cut your budget by $100,000 next quarter, find a way to do it that minimizes the damage to your team members, such as cutting back on discretionary expenditures, travel, and bonuses instead of cutting valued staff.

In a world where business competition has reached all the way into the boardroom, you have no choice but to stay alert for those who want to swoop down and steal your resources—whether that makes sense for the company or not. When presented with shortages, some people panic and do anything they can to stay on top.

So keep your eyes open, stay calm, and block any unwise attempts to take you or your team down. Be a team player for the organization, but verbalize your needs and stand up for your rights without shirking.

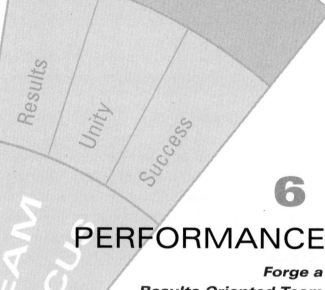

Results

Unity

Success

TEAM
FOCUS

6

PERFORMANCE

Forge a
Results-Oriented Team

In today's sped-up business environment, style is less likely than ever to triumph over substance. Results—not just staying busy—define productivity, while acting as a benchmark for new efforts. And producing results is at the heart of what it means to be efficient and effective.

The best workplace teams are so close-knit and results-oriented that productivity is a given. Such cohesion depends on trust and mutual respect, factors that naturally boost productivity. Everyone on the team must act as integral and active parts of that team; you can't allow cubicle hermits and slackers. Move forward with positive energy, developing the talents of your team members so you'll inevitably enhance performance.

Oddly enough, a few rough edges can help you generate the creativity and innovation that boost productivity to even

higher levels. But be careful to manage any disagreements between team members that result, so they don't spiral out of
control.

There may be times when you'll have to be ruthless to revitalize your team, clearing out true "deadwood"—specifically,
negative attitudes and unprofitable processes—rather than people. This might require a shot of SWOT analysis (Strengths,
Weaknesses, Opportunities, and Threats), focusing on the big
picture of team productivity. So gear up for success through
a commitment to excellence, focused effort, and intelligent
planning.

CONSISTENT RESULTS: SUBSTANCE OVER STYLE

Perception creates reality in most people's minds, but this tendency can lead you astray. You might think a person with feet
up on the desk and eyes closed is wasting company time, as
did one efficiency expert hired by Henry Ford. Ford informed
the expert that the man had once had an idea that saved Ford
millions of dollars, and he noted, "At the time, I believe his
feet were planted right where they are now."[23]

A Modest Proposal

You set the tone for your team, so make a commitment to put
substance over style. Refuse to lock your team into rigid ways
of thinking and doing, in which the company line matters
more than the bottom line. Within ethical, moral, and legal
limits, do what benefits your organization most and gets you
closer to its goals. To wit:

1 **BREAK FREE FROM BUREAUCRACY.** Many organizations
settle on what they consider "best practices" and stay
there indefinitely. But "best" changes with technology and

culture. Don't become so hardened that you refuse to take advantage of new "bests" as they become available and the old bests become outdated.

2 **STOP CONFUSING "BUSY" WITH "PRODUCTIVE."** Who cares how many items you cross off your list if you accomplish nothing worthwhile? Put your priority items at the top of your list and do those *first*, even if they take hours. If you and your team get only three items done in a day but earn the company $100,000, you've beaten the pants off the drones who rushed around doing thirty minor items and never managed to get to their most important tasks, thus earning nothing.

3 **WORK *ON* YOUR BUSINESS, NOT *IN* IT.** You're an executive, so your actions should make your team's work easier, improve the workflow, build profitable bridges with other teams and organizations, intercept red tape, and accomplish other substantial tasks. Leave the day-to-day tasks where they belong—with your team. It doesn't matter how busy you look. Trying to wear all the hats and working *in* your business, rather than working *on* it, gets nothing done that others couldn't accomplish at a lower salary.

4 **STOP TRYING TO IMPRESS PEOPLE WITH YOUR PERSONAL STYLE.** This applies to your fashion sense or how you approach your job. Impress them instead with your acumen and productivity. Apple's Steve Jobs often wore casual clothing, even to meetings with important shareholders. Did his fashion sense make him any less impressive? Of course not. His ability to turn vision into reality, choose inventive people to create products the public wanted, and

infect others with his sense of productivity mattered—not his clothing choices.

5 **DON'T LET STYLE BLIND YOU TO ABILITY.** Make sure you aren't judging books by their covers when you size up your employees' abilities. Just because someone looks like an alpha geek doesn't mean he's your best choice as a programmer, any more than another person's odd working schedule automatically makes him a slacker. Business professor Alex Taylor tells the story of a hiring manager who realized that the irregular hours of an otherwise exemplary employee were due to her being a single mother struggling to fit her child's needs around a traditional schedule. When he put her in a position with a schedule that specifically matched her needs, she became one of the best employees he'd ever managed.[24]

Beyond the Superficial

It's human nature to accept that "what we see is what we get." That's a relic of the caveman days. But in the modern era, people usually have time to think before they react. So don't let what's on the surface blind you; look through it to see what lies beneath, acting on that instead.

The True Measure of Productivity

No amount of planning matters if you fail to couple it with firm, decisive action. It doesn't matter how many tiger team meetings you attend, whether or not you're ISO compliant, or that you got an enthusiastic thumbs-up on your trust exercises during that last retreat.

What matters is this: can you and your team consistently produce at a high level, meeting or exceeding your goals before reaching out for new ones? If not, something's broken in your workflow process, and you must repair it immediately. Without productivity, and the dollars it brings in, your organization won't survive.

Recoupling Performance and Reality

If you've heard it once, you've heard it a hundred times: what you can't measure, you can't improve. Set up some way to measure not only team performance but each team member's individual performance as well. You have many potential ways to go about it. Here are some suggestions:

- *Balanced scorecards* are standardized reports generated by software tools that track individual and group performance. While the reports can prove useful, they depend on team members accurately reporting time spent on each task, and on you paying close attention to reality as opposed to what the reports are telling you.

- *Scoreboards and dashboards* are automated software tools that provide aggregate data for key performance indicators specific to the organization or task. For example, a company that makes cotton candy may want to know how many pounds each employee produces per hour, either precisely or on average. Monitoring other factors, such as sugar usage, tons shipped, and packaging used may also help generate ideas to improve productivity.

- *Periodic performance reviews* work well for individual employees, helping both you and them understand how well they're doing on the productivity front, and what they need to improve upon. Most organizations focus on yearly reviews associated with performance raises or bonuses, but twice-yearly or quarterly reviews may be more effective for boosting productivity, along with monthly informal coaching sessions.

- *Business performance management* includes a series of activities intended to manage teams as they work toward achieving specific goals. It consists primarily of selection of goals, consolidation of relevant management information, and intervention intended to improve future performance.

- *Team dynamics reviews* help you clarify how your team members work together. In addition to personal observation and coaching, tools such as Myers-Briggs personality tests and 360-degree feedback provide valuable clues on how to interact with team members. They can help you forestall any potential problems.

Talk Is Cheap

Actions speak louder than words. Performance and productivity always matter more than talking a good game, so all efforts toward enhancing results should be rewarded and encouraged.

If your team focus has fallen short, help your employees get back on the ball by challenging them, inspiring them, and affirming their worth. Know when to step in and be a true leader—someone who won't *let* them fail. To paraphrase Vince Lombardi's famous line, "Performance isn't everything, it's the only thing."

Once you've gotten your team's buy-in and engaged their belief, try one of the measurement methods I've suggested to gauge, maintain, and control their performance.

ENCOURAGING TEAM UNITY

Cohesive teams are more productive than those with internal problems or those that simply aren't on the same page at all times. It's up to you to enhance your team's performance by holding them together in every way possible.

The Leader as Teammate

Most people respect authority, responding positively and productively to it. However, the modern concept of teamwork requires you not only to captain the ship but to be an active part of the crew as well.

Open Door or Closed?

Traditionally, leaders have kept themselves separate from their subordinates to ensure fairness. Yet distancing yourself from your team can damage cohesion and team unity. Some management experts have advocated an "open door" policy for years because of this.

So the question is, how do you remain accessible to your team while remaining fair and maintaining privacy? Where should *you* strike the balance? Here are three general guidelines that work well for me and my clients:

1 KNOW THE DIFFERENCE BETWEEN AVAILABILITY AND ACCESSIBILITY. Being completely available ties you down and makes you a less effective leader. If you're always available, then you always have to stay where someone can find you. That also means you'll be interrupted all day long and will have to do your "real work" after everyone else leaves.

Instead, be *accessible*, not fully available. Don't keep your door open all day. Encourage team members to schedule appointments, not just "pop in." Let them know when you're available for coaching. Schedule regular meetings with key players, so they don't feel the need to interrupt you with questions. Work team members in around your schedule when they need you. Remember, being accessible for your team is part of your job, not an inconvenience; defining boundaries will help you treat it that way.

2 **FILTER YOUR PERSONAL ACCESS.** If you get too many requests for your time, you may need to adopt a filtering system to limit access to you. This could take the form of what I call "a dragon at the gate"—a tough executive assistant who handles most requests and passes the remainder on to you directly. If you've reached the C-Suite, you may need several people to fill this role.

3 **SET OFFICE HOURS.** Establish hours during the week when anyone can approach you with questions or problems, for example, Tuesday through Thursday, 1 to 3 P.M. This limits your need to stay in one place while still making you available. You can also leverage the concept of reverse office hours—times when you *never* make yourself available so you can get work done.

He Said, She Said—A Simple Mediation Process

In any group, you'll have conflict. In most cases, you can all sit down and reach a reasonable agreement after a give-and-take discussion—assuming everyone wants to work it out. If the disagreement seems petty, make a quick decision and get everyone back to work fast. But some conflicts are too deep-rooted or antagonistic to dismiss so readily. In those situations, turn to a set of mediation tools you can pick up and put to work on the issue. These tools don't work in every situation, but I find the following tips help me clear up most conflicts between others, in business and in life:

1 **RESEARCH THE ISSUE.** Don't go into the situation blind. Know the background and have some idea of how you can clear the roadblock, based on how others have handled similar situations. If you don't have much mediation experience, brush up on the basics before you get started.

2 **MEET WITH THE CONFLICTING PARTIES.** Some mediation experts tell you never to meet with the conflicting parties separately, because it generates mistrust. Others insist it's necessary to do this first to get each person's side of the story —a strategy I agree with. But if this step makes you uncomfortable, skip it and meet with the conflicting parties together.

While you're meeting, ask each party, one at a time, to present their side of the issue, assuring them they can do so uninterrupted. Enforce that promise, even if one of them tries to break in. Once both have presented their cases, summarize the situation as you understand it. Ask what each person *specifically* wants from the other(s) to resolve the conflict.

3 **INVESTIGATE THE RELIABILITY OF THE PARTIES.** Double-check the information you've received. Research the incidents mentioned by the parties, check into their allegations, and, if necessary, ask other coworkers about the incident. Consider the reputations of those involved, taking previous actions and conflicts into account. All this may give you a handle on the situation that will let you

resolve it more quickly. But if it doesn't, think deeply about what your investigations and interviews with the conflicting parties have revealed. Give yourself long enough for the information to percolate through your subconscious. You might find a way to render a decision at that point.

4 **FORGE AN AGREEMENT.** If you can hammer out a solution at this point, great. If not, at least try to get the parties to agree to further negotiation, so you can put the situation behind you as cleanly and as quickly as possible. Repeat as necessary.

You can handle relatively minor situations quickly and fairly with this process, especially when dealing with issues that boil down to personality clashes or spats over resources. If it doesn't produce results, though, call in human resources or a mediation expert. You can't referee employee disputes full-time.

Regardless of how you decide to handle a dispute, act immediately. Never let the problem fester. If you do, it may affect your entire team, dragging others in and forcing them to take sides. The longer you wait, the more work it will take to fix the problem. So when coworker friction starts emitting smoke, step in and deal with it right away—before it ignites a fire you can't handle.

Speaking of Fires . . .

Sometimes setting a motivational fire within the team can be useful if it jolts people out of complacency—or sheer laziness—and gets them back to work. Since teamwork rules in the business environment, having team members who don't shoulder their share of the load can jam the work process gears, bringing productivity to a halt. Slackers slow team efficiency, and they infect others with their bad attitudes as well. Once you recognize poor behavior, you'll need to get things moving again.

Springing into Action

Now, when you identify slackers, don't automatically assume they realize what's happening. Their poor work may not be deliberate. They may be so worried about something at home they can't do a good job at work. Possibly, they lack the right training to do as well as they should. Perhaps they're overwhelmed, not a good fit for their jobs, or bored. Maybe they don't recognize their own incompetence. So before lowering the boom, start with these corrective actions:

1 **BE HONEST WITH THEM.** Call them into your office and alert them to your concerns, pointing out specific examples. Ask, "Is there something going on I should know about?" This might be all you need to do to snap them out of whatever's been holding them back. It may be a difficult conversation to have, especially if you haven't already made an effort to get to know the team member. They might not be willing to open up to you, but try anyway.

Once you've pinpointed the problem, work on it. If they don't understand the requirements of the workplace, teach them what they need to know about the organization, the team, and the goals everyone needs to achieve. Provide the training they need. Pair them with a mentor.

Be prepared for slackers who know exactly what they're doing. They may have deliberately pushed the edges of the envelope to see what they could get away with or be actively hostile. If so, move to the next step.

2 **PUT THEM ON NOTICE.** How you put an underperformer on notice depends on the cause of the problem. If something in their life is distracting them, offer poor performers potential solutions. But unless it's a matter of life and death, also insist they find a way to work it out so they can do the minimum requirements of their job. If they can't, or it *does* involve a matter of life and death, suggest they take time off to deal with it. You can replace them with temp workers until they feel ready to return. Human resources may need to be involved here to navigate any issues of employee and employer rights.

If the unproductive employees behave in hostile, demanding, misguided, or lazy ways, don't play the game. Appraise them carefully, document the corrective action, and give them milestones they have to meet to get back on track and off probation.

3 **MOTIVATE THEM.** Once you've put underperformers on notice, don't disappear until reassessment time. Keep an eye on them and find ways to motivate them to do a better job. Perhaps provide an outside coach. Make sure they understand what their job entails and why it's important in both team and organizational contexts. Try small rewards for successful completion of milestone tasks. It could even be something as minor as a certificate of achievement or a Starbucks gift card with a handwritten note—whatever's in your power to give. If nothing else works, it's time for:

4 **THE NUCLEAR OPTION.** If it's not working out, invite underperformers to explore their talents elsewhere. Jack Welch, former CEO of GE, famously fired the bottom 10 percent of performers in his company every year. He received a lot of criticism for it, but no one can deny that GE thrived under his guidance.

Enough's Enough

Slackers are productivity vampires, slowly draining your team of life. The worst of them blame others for their faults, express a toxic attitude, and deliberately stir up trouble.

Immediately respond to them by putting them on notice. Find ways to engage and motivate them where possible—and the sooner the better. If things don't clear up relatively quickly, show them the door for your team's sake.

SUCCESS BASED ON BUILDING STRENGTHS AND REDUCING WEAKNESSES

Even if you're not part of a problem, you have to make a sincere effort to be part of the solution. No matter how well you run your own team, you'll have weaknesses that can undermine your strengths if you're not careful. I believe in maximizing strengths rather than focusing on weaknesses, but at the same time, you should know your weaknesses so you can work around them—and root them out whenever possible. I recommend the following process:

1 **CONDUCT A CLASSIC SWOT ANALYSIS.** Pretend you're back in Business Analysis 101 and list your team's Strengths, Weaknesses, Opportunities, and Threats. It needn't take long, but do put sincere effort into it. Dig deeper than the obvious, and consider your options thoroughly.

2 **CONSULT YOUR TEAM.** As a leader, you may have different ideas of what constitutes a weakness than your team does, so ask your people to contribute their ideas.

Sometimes this works wonders. During experiments in 2005 and 2006, Best Buy Vice President Jeff Severts discovered that delegating sales forecasts to Best Buy employees produced better results than consulting a team of professional experts, on an order of up to 4.5 to 7 percent. Why? Probably because of the diversity of staff forecasters and because the employees actually used the products the company sold.[25]

3 **AUDIT THE BIG PICTURE.** Do you have happy customers? How's your productivity rate? Is there black or red ink on the bottom line? Do your processes flow smoothly, or do they hinder productivity? Does your team structure work? How can you be more effective? Don't ignore the big picture in favor of minor issues, or get caught up in the daily minutiae, even briefly. Look around often. Make sure an unexpected change or threat doesn't run you down.

4 **RESPOND WELL TO FEEDBACK.** Don't blow off criticisms, constructive or otherwise, especially when they come from within. Rather, invite them. When I was the president of the National Speakers Association in 2011, a couple of board members privately pulled me aside and gave me tips on how to run meetings more efficiently, which I really appreciated. When you know where the holes are, you can plug them before your ship sinks.

5 **LOOK AT *EVERYTHING*.** Weaknesses are not necessarily obvious; they might not even look like weaknesses at first. Suppose you pride yourself on putting out a great monthly newsletter for your clients. Are they reading it and receiving value from it? What would happen if you stopped producing it? The case study here is me. After an illness a couple of years ago, I didn't put out my monthly newsletter one month, and only three people noticed. A little investigation revealed that my clients thought my newsletter was informative but too long. All they wanted was a brief tip weekly. Suddenly, I found a previously unknown weakness and was able to replace it with something more impactful and less time-consuming.

Most of all, remain objective. Once you've conducted your SWOT exercise and examined team performance, you may find you have little or nothing to worry about. Great! But that doesn't mean you can rest on your laurels. Note not only where you are and where you've been, but where you want to be in the near future. Complacency can kill as quickly as incompetence.

Engineer a Quantum Leap in Productivity

In physics, the term "quantum leap" refers to an electron's sudden jump to a higher energy state without passing through the distance in between. It's such an attractive notion that people have taken to using the term "quantum leap" when referring to any spectacular feat.

Quantum effects can't *really* manifest at human scales, but this is great shorthand for a sudden improvement in performance or productivity. However, unlike an electron's quantum leap, the human productivity equivalent leaves a trail.

Put the Situation under a Microscope

Take a close look at every aspect of your team and workplace setting you can think of: the players, your projects, what's coming over the horizon, your productivity level, your processes and workflow system, your tools and applications, the other groups you interact with, the environment. Given these factors, how would you rate your condition: average, below average, or above average?

What Would a Quantum Leap Look Like?

A quantum leap wouldn't be a simple improvement—it would be a massive overhaul in how you do something, maybe even a new technology or process. Determine what big productivity step you would take if you could. Paint a picture of the ideal productive workforce of the future.

Partner on the Mission

Get your team together and share this vision of the future. Explain your ideas and request assistance from your teammates. Ask them what would need to happen to make it a reality. Brainstorm with them about how you could magically jump to that place. Explain that you see this meeting as a springboard for bigger and better things, and get them caught up in the mission.

Create the Roadmap

Begin by documenting the specific goals you have to meet by drawing a "treasure map." The goals should be big enough to see from a great distance and far enough away that everyone has to stretch to reach them. Agree on where you are now with a big X, and then agree on the changes that have to occur.

Back in the 1970s, Bill Gates and Steve Jobs set out to change the world of computing by making its power available to everyday people—a quantum leap in technology. In the personas of their companies, Microsoft and Apple, both of them could see the future. They had a good idea of how to get there, and their teams helped achieve it, point by point.

Remember to SWOT the challenges. Use the SWOT method outlined in the previous section to pencil in on your treasure map the "mountain ranges" and "rivers" (threats) that will block your progress. Should you go around them or power straight through? *Can* you power through? Why not? Who or what will stop you? This is a team exercise, so keep your people involved with every step. Some may surprise you with their suggestions.

Start the Bulldozer

Your role makes you a visionary and a facilitator—noble responsibilities no matter how you slice them. As a facilitator, you have the honor of making it easier for people to follow your lead and do their jobs. In a way, you're like a bulldozer, smoothing the way, filling in potholes, and clearing out trees and stumps that might slow your team down. This may mean acquiring training for everyone who needs it or providing new phones or upgraded software—whatever it takes to make their lives easier and their work more profitable.

Remember: there's no such thing as the perfect time for anything. And if you wait for that nonexistent perfect time, you may never begin. This process will help your team take a quantum leap toward productivity stardom.

7

MOTIVATION

Harness Creativity and Loyalty

Individual engagement and empowerment drive workplace productivity, even
at the team level. Effective leaders must
internalize the factors motivating their team
members, so they can use their tools in the best
way possible to boost productivity.

As noted earlier, emphasize the value of your team
members' contributions, showing them how everyone
contributes to the success of the entire team. Invite your
team on this journey by motivating them and empowering
them as your partners in success. Ask for and consider their
ideas and opinions.

Take hold of your own creativity, finding ways to harness it
and passing those ideas on to your team members. And never
lose sight of the fact that they *are* your teammates; you're a
team member, not just a leader.

Always seek employee loyalty. This won't come naturally,

115

so encourage it through basic managerial tactics, avoiding micromanagement, and being tough but fair. Most importantly, demonstrate your gratitude for a job well done and encourage team trust, tightening team cohesion at every turn.

ENSURING TEAM-MEMBER ENGAGEMENT

Those of us who've worked in an environment in which leaders actively encourage engagement can testify to its effectiveness.

The basic recipe for ensuring engagement is surprisingly simple, though the ingredients and precise amounts needed can vary according to the workplace and team. Include these factors in your engagement initiatives:

- Knowledge of the organization's strategic goals.
- Clarification of each employee's place within that framework, and why their work matters.
- Sincere and explicit encouragement to take the initiative.
- Ability to take initiative without unreasonable censure.
- Willingness to trust the workers.
- Delegation of authority as well as tasks and duties.
- Refusal to micromanage.
- Respect for all team members and what they do.
- Strong leadership through action and example.
- Positive motivation in forms advantageous to the team.

The last point may be the most important ingredient in engagement. People are more willing to own their jobs and invest more discretionary effort if there's a payoff, though it doesn't have to be monetary. As media mogul Rupert Murdoch once pointed out, "In motivating people, you've got to engage their minds and their hearts. I motivate people, I hope, by example—and perhaps by excitement, by having productive ideas to make others feel involved."

Lost Chances

According to the spring 2013 National Employee Engagement Study by Modern Survey, employee engagement levels in the United States had dropped to their lowest rates in six years at that point.[26] Thirty-two percent of the one thousand workers surveyed rated themselves completely disengaged, with only 10 percent fully engaged and another 22 percent moderately engaged. The rest were underengaged.

Fortunately, by fall 2014, the numbers had improved to 22 percent disengaged, 28 percent moderately engaged, 16 percent fully engaged, and 35 percent underengaged.[27] But these numbers are still dismal, especially in an era of economic uncertainty like ours. What gives?

In the spring 2013 study, Modern Survey concluded that a big part of the problem was that half of all employees (including managers!) simply *didn't know what engagement meant.* No one had ever bothered to explain it to them, much less point out why it matters. Among those who did know what it meant—63 percent of managers versus 43 percent of nonmanagement employees—the big issue was that no one understood engagement's primary drivers. Worse, most had no idea who bore the responsibility for taking ownership of engagement: was it employees, managers, or senior leadership?

Only 39 percent knew the truth: that ownership of engagement belongs to all of the above.[28] That might seem simplistic, but that makes it no less true. It's in everyone's best interests for an employee to *want* to take ownership of his or her job. But too often, front-line workers don't even know they have the right to do so.

Too many people have worked for companies with rigid hierarchies and permission-based cultures, so it should come as no surprise that most workers engage only when directly told to do so. It's your duty, then, to reeducate your employees so they realize they can take the initiative. Let them know you prefer it!

Shouldering Your Share

You not only have to make it explicitly obvious to your people that they have permission to take the initiative, but you also have to give them reasons to care.

Sure, you can spend months defining your core values, articulating mission and vision, and fashioning a flexible, up-to-the-minute strategy, but if your team's collective attitude boils down to "Who cares?" or simple disbelief, then you've lost the game before you've even begun. If that's true, then no one's at fault but you, no matter who you want to blame. So work hard to engage your team and rev their motivational engines.

Start by showing them you believe in them, and that you will hold them to a higher standard because you have confidence they can achieve it. Try these five tips, especially when the going gets tough:

1 **MAKE SURE THEY UNDERSTAND THE BIG PICTURE.**
   If your team isn't already familiar with the organization's main goals, lay them out in plain language. Make sure they feel valued within that big picture, so they'll have reason to feel they "own" their jobs.

2 **GIVE THEM WHAT THEY NEED.** I can't repeat this enough. If your employees lack the right tools or training, they may not feel capable of or confident about doing the tasks you've assigned them. Whether they need training, a new computer, a smartphone, or a better printer, make it happen, so they can move forward with confidence.

3 **PLAN CAREFULLY.** Collaborate with your team on how to best achieve long-term goals. Review the plans and get everyone involved in how to proceed. Give them active, important roles in building those plans, as well as in controlling deadlines, scheduling, project management, and scope creep. Establish performance goals. Provide reasonable objectives for team members to shoot for, both as individuals and as a team, but make everyone stretch a little to reach them.

4 **PROVIDE TRACKING METRICS.** Show your team how they're doing. If they realize they're the front-runners in a company-wide sales race, they may work hard to stay there. Or if they're in second place, they may redouble their efforts to take first place. Consider it a report card for the team, one that may inspire them to kick it into high gear.

5 **CELEBRATE SUCCESSES.** When something goes right, even something small, make sure your team knows you appreciate their efforts. Public pats on the back are cheap and, in some cases, just as effective as cash. You can also provide treats for the break room or take everyone to lunch when things go well. If a project's especially important or difficult, promise your folks that, when they complete it—

especially if it comes in early and under budget—you'll have a blowout party, or they'll get a special treat such as a three-day weekend. Give them something to strive for.

Intrinsic and Extrinsic Rewards

You already know that dangling the carrot of a bonus, raise, or promotion works wonders for some people. But those are individual prizes, not team ones. Intrinsic rewards, on the other hand, can act as powerful motivators in team environments. The thrill of reaching a difficult goal can be its own reward. Knowing how to motivate your team with the intrinsic satisfaction of meeting challenges and doing exceptional work gives you another strategy to keep them at the top of their game. And even if someone is determined to be the MVP, that person still pulls the entire team upward. As basketball great Michael Jordan once pointed out, there's no "I" in "team," but there is in "win."

The ABCs of Motivation

Brian Halligan, CEO of the online marketing firm HubSpot, has a singular way of handling go-getter employees who present him with great ideas with the potential to improve the company's bottom line. He fires them.

The punchline? He then appoints them as the CEOs of their own change initiatives, akin to little start-ups within the company. Halligan calls this his Mini-CEO Program, and he does it to both decentralize the company and empower team players.[29] You can bet it motivates the heck out of his employees to do their best for him, so they'll have a shot at the big time.

What can you do to motivate your employees? With fewer than 25 percent of nonmanagerial employees fully engaged in their jobs,[30] those in the catbird seats have unique opportunities to dangle similar carrots before their team members. Helping them help themselves by devoting themselves more fully to their careers is a win/win situation. There's no altruism here: fully engaged employees, who are passionate about their work, keep team and organizational performance trending steadily upward.

Truth is, you can't really motivate people to do anything; they have to motivate themselves. But you can provide incentives and an environment people find motivating, so they're inspired to contribute their discretionary efforts.

It's as easy as ABC—and DEF:

A = Analyze. Everyone's different, so determine what each person wants in return for extra discretionary effort. Give them all the opportunity to profit when the company does. For example, offer flexible scheduling, raises, bonuses, conference attendance, part-time telecommuting, certificates, or pats on the back—whatever it takes. Another A-word, Awards, is your friend here. But don't hand them out indiscriminately. Give them only to those who fully deserve them.

B = Balance. Your team members need a good work/life balance to remain productive. At a certain point (about the tenth hour of a long workday), accumulated error and declining performance overwhelm any benefit derived from continuing to work. Make sure everyone gets the rest and the breaks they need—from daily coffee to their annual vacations—and they'll take care of you. Be a good role model as well. If you send an email at 2 A.M. when you have insomnia, be sure to let the recipient know you don't expect anyone to be working that late!

C = Communicate. We use the gift of gab for a reason: it's still the best way we've invented to convey ideas. Explain what you need everyone to do and why—clearly, plainly, and honestly. Each week, my office manager and I review her master list to prioritize her tasks for the next few days. We make sure we're on the same page, and then I get out of her way and let her do her job. Keep the lines open for whenever a team member needs assistance.

D = Direction. Although the manager's role has changed in the last few decades, leaders are still responsible for providing the team's mission and vision. You'll see better results when you strategically align individual and team goals with their organizational counterparts. Performance management is one of the most important areas of motivation, since it produces significant improvement if you can implement it. Review milestones and provide coaching with each of your direct reports in weekly one-on-one meetings. Show them why you can't get there without their help.

E = Expect. Let your people know what you expect from them as unambiguously as possible. But if someone discovers a better way of getting from here to there, let them take it—as long as it's ethical and legal. Expect great things from your team and model those expectations in your own behavior.

F = Facilitate. When you make it easier for your team to succeed, you boost their morale, performance, and productivity. Go out ahead of everyone and demolish the bureaucratic hurdles, fill in the technological potholes, and build bridges to span knowledge gaps. Influence senior leaders to get the budget you need. Run interference if another department is slowing your team down. When your team sees you out there fighting for them by providing the assistance they need to improve, they can't help but want to do their best for you.

If you give your team members valid, easy-to-understand reasons to do well, you'll push productivity through the roof. This little lexicon just scratches the surface of the various ways you can motivate your people to shine. There are twenty more letters to explore, and most have more than one word to draw upon.

HARNESSING CREATIVITY

Allowing your team to unleash their creativity on your collective business problems is an excellent way to motivate them to donate their discretionary effort to the organization. It costs you nothing extra, except for a willingness to relinquish absolute control of your team, and it can deeply benefit your organization.

So encourage your people to think of novel ways to boost the company's profit. It's in everyone's interest, it's cheap, and, as with Forrest Gump's box of chocolates, "you never know what you're gonna get."

Consider these four suggestions for combining creativity with your work processes:

1 SET ASIDE TIME FOR CREATIVITY. You may have heard of a little company called Google. According to company rules, employees can spend up to 20 percent of their time working on personal projects they feel can boost the company's profitability (although former executive Marissa Mayer, now CEO of Yahoo, has stated that it was really only practiced above and beyond the normal workweek—

"120 percent," as she put it). The practice has earned Google millions. Outcomes include Gmail, AdSense, and Google News.[31] You may not be able to give your people a full day off every week to pursue personal projects, but even the occasional half hour spent brainstorming can have a positive effect on team productivity.

2 **STUDY OTHER DISCIPLINES.** In nature, some of the toughest plants and animals are crossbreeds. They tend to be healthier than purebreds, because inbreeding reinforces bad genes, producing more duds than random breeding. The same goes for business ideas. Read widely about success-ful people and businesses in a variety of fields, stay aware of scientific progress in fields other than your own—and keep your eyes open. Encourage your people to do the same.

3 **LISTEN TO YOUR TEAM'S IDEAS AND ADVICE.** Your team has combined experience measured in decades. Some of that experience may be superior to your own in certain areas. Take advantage of it, urging everyone to make suggestions about how to better achieve company or team goals. If they prefer to stay mum, offer a reward for profitable ideas. You may jostle a few loose. And remember: your team's ideas may be like seedlings. When they first emerge, you never know which will die off, which will be weeds, or which will grow into mighty oaks that buttress your organization's suc-cess. So give ideas time to mature before you thin them out.

4 **DON'T PUNISH FAILURE.** Everyone makes mistakes or overestimates the worth of some ideas or initiatives. Most ideas fail. Some fail dismally. Let your people err with-out worrying about punishment. Otherwise, they may give up too soon. There's an old joke about someone's uncle who invented 1-Up through 6-Up and then GAVE up. Though humorous, it teaches a sly lesson about tenacity. Many famous entrepreneurs failed multiple times in their careers before striking it rich.

While we have procedures and traditions for a reason, we can't let them hold us back. Mavericks who keep their eyes open and are willing to try something new drive innovation. So open your eyes to the possibilities. As the saying goes, in the land of the blind, the one-eyed man is king. Imagine how well you can do with *both* eyes open.

ACHIEVING SUCCESS THROUGH LOYALTY

In recent years, I've repeatedly seen business leaders bemoan the death of employee loyalty. This amazes me every time I hear it because, really, why would anyone be surprised? This loss is completely predictable.

On the one hand, technology has freed employees from most traditional workplace restraints. Some have decided to strike out on their own; others realize they can get further faster by jumping from company to company instead of working their way through the hierarchy of one organization. On the other hand, global competition and shareholder demands have ensured that most companies can no longer provide life-long employment or traditional pensions—loyalty guarantees that workers once took for granted. So why *should* employees feel loyal toward the company?

The New Loyalty Paradigm

That said, employee loyalty need not be a thing of the past. No one expects lifelong loyalty anymore, but you can increase loyalty to gratifying levels if you make a few adjustments to the way you do business.

A simple way is to treat your team with trust and respect. One of your chief aims should be to make your team's work easier by clearing the way toward achieving your goals. Respect your people by making those goals crystal clear and show them you're working as hard as they are. Don't look down on your teammates or dismiss their concerns. Give them the training and advice they need to do their jobs well. Shared respect takes many routes, and you have to police them all.

Strive for consistency along the way. Workers need to be able to predict your behavior, at least to some extent, and know you'll treat everyone the same way no matter what. Otherwise, how can they trust you? When you make a promise, fulfill it. Follow through with your commitments. If a specific achievement earns a specific award, everyone who captures that achievement gets the award. Display consistency with word and deed, and expect the same of your people. They'll respect you for it.

Empower your team. Let your team members own their jobs. If they can function without excess interference or overly punitive responses to mistakes, they'll stay with you longer. Give them room to breathe, and let them take the initiative to improve their own output. They'll find it easier to execute strategy at a moment's notice if they don't always have to ask permission first.

Above all, lead! Your position gives you the ability to shape other people's lives by example. Your workers watch you constantly, so they know if you ignore your own rules. Leadership means more than ordering people around; it means guidance, in everything from coaching to living up to your promises.

Looking Ahead

Accept the fact that business has changed irrevocably due to technological and sociological evolution. No matter where you work or what you do, team members will leave more often than you like, and you'll be forced to bring newbies up to speed. Even innovative companies such as Amazon and Google have higher turnover rates than you'd expect.[32] You can't hold on to people as your predecessors did, but that doesn't mean you shouldn't try. While money and position mean a great deal to employees, so do simple things including trust, compassion, respect, empowerment, good communications, and solid leadership.

The Power of Gratitude

Good old-fashioned appreciation can be amazingly motivational and loyalty-inducing. Shortly after Robert Eckert joined the ailing toy company Mattel as CEO back in 2000, he convened a meeting of all its employees to thank them all for their fine work—and for the even finer work they were about to do.

Eckert let them know he believed most people go to work willing to overdeliver. From that foundational belief, a culture of gratitude sprang forth, helping Mattel become the envy of the manufacturing industry. While it took a few years to turn the company around, Mattel made the Top 100 in *Fortune*'s list of the "Best Companies to Work For" from 2008 through 2013.[33]

Adding an Attitude of Gratitude to Your Business

How can *you* sow the seeds of a gratitude culture within your team? Consider these factors while handing out thanks:

1 **DON'T OVERDO IT.** Praising everyone for everything they do dilutes the effect. One of my friends is a ghostwriter, and for years, he had a customer who praised everything he submitted to the skies. While my friend appreciated that, and no doubt the customer meant it, the praise became routine and expected—until the customer had to pare back his business and stopped sending my friend more work. In some ways, that effusive praise meant less than praise from tougher clients who were perfectly willing to bounce an article back for rewrite—or even kill it—if it didn't meet their needs.

2 **BE GENUINE.** Don't always couch praise as a warm-up to criticism. If you inevitably follow praise with correction, employees will think of your gratitude as a platitude. When they hear positive words, they'll think, "Here it comes," in anticipation of the critique that is sure to follow. Instead, sincerely praise what employees have done right. Even if they made mistakes, you can preface coaching with an appreciation of their willingness to take on the task and learn new things.

3 **GIVE GIFTS.** For many people, nothing works better as a motivator than a simple "thank you" and a pat on the back. And while verbal praise is important, we all respond positively to tangible gifts. In multilevel marketing, the smart recruiters *always* thank their recruits, especially party-planning hosts, with a worthwhile gift. Gifts not only encourage people to repeat desired behavior, they also trigger the reciprocity effect—when you do something nice for someone, they feel the need to do something nice for you.[34] A well-timed gift may encourage your people to go above and beyond on the next project.

4 **RECOGNIZE MILESTONES.** A monthly party with a cake for that month's birthdays is an inexpensive way to build camaraderie. Other important team milestones may include surpassing a sales benchmark, hitting a five- or ten-year anniversary with the company, or far exceeding expectations—so make sure they get the recognition they deserve. Recognition differs from praise because you do it in public.

As he explained to me in an interview, Senior Vice President Darren Smith's recipe for company loyalty at John Hancock Investments is simple, straightforward, and includes all these strategies. He keeps good people on board by

very thoughtfully and intentionally fostering a culture of excellence that is people focused, family friendly, and performance driven. This can't just be a slogan that hangs on the wall, but has to become part of the corporate DNA, present in all that we do. You have to start with a foundation of cultural integrity, which essentially means that we are who we say we are, and we do what we say we'll do.

We believe that a company can and does have a soul, and it is evidenced in the company's culture. If we have achieved true cultural integrity, then that culture should be manifested in the same way from the top to the bottom of the organization. Once the cultural foundation is in place, respect, recognition, and appreciation provide constant reinforcement and are crucial in developing loyalty. Recognition should come not only in the form of corporate trophies at the year-end, but also in personal touches on a regular basis.

Those touches take a number of different forms, to

include verbal affirmations, inclusion, monetary recognition, and birthday, anniversary, and holiday greetings.
Study after study has shown that the biggest factor in
employee loyalty is appreciation, and if we can get that
right, we rarely lose people.

Paying It Forward

Gratitude is like the magic penny from the kids' song: the
more you give it away, the richer you become. Expressing
appreciation—and really meaning it—will make a huge difference. Your employees will feel proud that you've acknowl-
edged their efforts. Never take them for granted.

The words in the fan graphic: Stretch, Accountability, Conflict, TEAM FOCUS

8

GROWTH

Emphasize
Continuous
Improvement

We all have to grow into our jobs, whether we're bike messengers or CEOs. Once you've built and shaped your team members into a vehicle for true productivity, focus on finding ways to optimize their performance through further growth. Effective, efficient execution is not a fixed destination; it is a moving target that can only be hit consistently if you and your team are seeking ways to constantly improve.

Growing together as a team and growing to *become* a team creates cohesion—with individual team members interlocking smoothly into one efficient entity like the parts of a good machine or jigsaw puzzle. A mature team develops features that naturally boost productivity. But the effort starts with you, the executive—whatever your job title. You can facilitate this process and avoid problems by understanding not only how *you* think but also how your team members think.

Among other things, a quality leader accepts both credit and blame when it's due. Leaders act on constructive criticism without overreacting to the pain that accompanies it, because they know it can offer insight into where growth is needed. And most who deliver such criticism are trying to help, however clueless or hurtful their words might seem to you at the moment. Using your emotional intelligence while balancing your head and heart serves you well here.

STRETCH EVERY DAY IN EVERY WAY

Growth occurs on all levels in an organization—or at least it should. Lack of growth may not result in death, but it does lead to stagnation, which causes damage or death in the long run. While you have to center growth on your team to best benefit the organization, individual growth at the leadership level and cross-team development also affect team growth. So let's look at all three.

Harnessing the Power of Metacognition

In his 1734 poem "An Essay on Man," Alexander Pope declared, "The proper study of Mankind is Man."[35]

We've taken this motto to heart as a species. We've made radical advances in everything from economics and sociology to engineering and medicine in the handful of centuries since. Our ability to think clearly—and our *willingness* to do so—has led us to cultural and social heights undreamed of in previous civilizations.

Even better, we possess the remarkable ability to evaluate our own thinking. With a little self-reflection, we can understand *how* and *why* we think the way we do. And when we know the "how" and the "why" of something, we can usually improve upon it.

As an intelligent leader, you can take advantage of meta-cognition not only to comprehend your thought processes but also to understand how those around you think.

No one knows you as well as you do. You can use this knowledge to engineer your work patterns for maximum effectiveness and efficiency. So, for example: if you find it hard to stay off the Internet, then turn off the wireless connection except when you absolutely need to connect. If music soothes you, listen to Bach or play instrumental music on your noise-reducing headphones. If you know your mental energy peak occurs two hours after lunch, save your toughest tasks for then so you can power through them.

The more you think about how you think, the more you can use your self-knowledge to improve your productivity and boost your professional growth.

Know Them, Too

Metacognition also provides hints about how other people think—hints you can leverage to improve team performance. Suppose one of your team members enjoys a specific type of work. Why not make her the point woman for that type of work whenever you can?

Think about how the people around you think, even as you think more about how *you* think. Then you'll be able to build a more effective collaboration—with a workflow process that produces like never before.

Whistling Up an Orchestra

Those who gravitate toward leadership (or create businesses as entrepreneurs) tend to be the independent type. It seems ironic, then, that humans achieve their highest levels of productivity only by coming together as teams.

Human beings are social creatures. Nearly everything worthwhile we've achieved has come about as a result of team effort. Even those perceived as lone-wolf geniuses—Einstein, Mozart, da Vinci, Jobs—worked in a collaborative field or surrounded themselves with talented people they could trust. Yale Divinity School's H. E. Luccock may have said it best when he pointed out, "No one can whistle a symphony. It takes an orchestra to play it."

Why We Bother

The greatest advantage of teamwork is that it achieves what individuals can't through the medium of cooperation. Making personal goals secondary to group goals may seem difficult, but it pays off for everyone in the end.

Instilling effective teamwork as one of the team's core values will make the team:

- *More efficient.* Typically, more efficient also means faster, since many hands make light work. Teamwork is much more efficient (and effective) when team members work together closely throughout the process. Many tasks have no clear-cut edges, so when people work separately, performing separate parts of a project in isolation and then piecing them together later, overlap and duplication may occur. On a team where the members inform each other of their progress, that's easier to avoid. Ongoing feedback also increases the quality of output during the planning, design, and implementation stages. The result is more robust, with multiple perspectives.

- *More reliant on multiple skill sets.* Even in specialized fields, the constant evolution of knowledge and increase in information makes it impossible to know everything about the field. It takes a lot longer to complete a project if one person has to know everything necessary to accomplish it. To make efficient progress, put together subject matter experts on different aspects of the field and have them tackle the project as a group.

That said, you can't be completely dependent on any one person. When an employee is sick or on vacation, someone else must pick up the slack and still get the work done on time. If only one person is working on a project and holds the keys to the kingdom, that project suffers until they return—and may even die in their absence.

- *Accountable.* Team membership encourages a sense of belonging, which often translates to a greater sense of ownership and accountability for the work. This is especially true when people respect each other and don't want to let the team down.

- *Synergetic.* Cohesive, closely fitting teams often prove greater than the sum of their parts, such that the results are out of proportion to the number of people involved. Consider composers Gilbert and Sullivan, innovators Jobs and Wozniak, or pioneers Brin and Page.

And The Beat Goes On

Close collaboration is vital to human achievement at *all* levels. Teamwork stands as one of the chief hallmarks of human accomplishment. So encourage and exploit people's tendency to work together for the common good, even if you prefer solitude. Collaboration is basic human nature, and it might be much easier to strengthen than you think.

MAKING ACCOUNTABILITY YOUR WATCHWORD

When you use *employer* thinking versus *employee* thinking—and you treat your business as your own—you and your teammates are more likely to be held accountable for what you do or fail to do.

Accountability means following through on your promises and accepting the consequences when things go wrong. Only professional victims blame other people when unforeseen circumstances trip them up. How accountable you hold yourself depends on the extent to which you refuse to blame others or extenuating factors when things go wrong. US President Harry S. Truman said it best: "The buck stops here."

Personal responsibility isn't always easy, even for hard-core, competent professionals. Indeed, it can be downright difficult when you're at fault for something and may lose your job or hurt your career by owning up to it. But taking responsibility is the honorable, professional thing to do and the proper stance to take.

I've encountered some telling examples of the difference between *employer* and *employee* thinking in my work. When I schedule speaking engagements, I send a ten-question survey to my client and ask them to send it to fifteen or twenty intended audience members. Their replies help me tailor my speech to their needs. One question I always ask is, "What is the number one thing you would have to change about yourself to become more productive?" A large number of the answers look like this:

- I'm too hot (or too cold).
- Nobody will give me the right training.
- I don't have the tools I need.
- Bad lighting.

Seriously? Bad lighting? That reflects not only an inability to read the question but astounding laziness. I keep thinking, "Okay, now I've heard it all," but I'm always wrong. Most people would rather make excuses than make a little effort to help themselves.

Come on, you're not a kid anymore. People won't make themselves responsible for your actions and the results that follow. And why should they?

If you lack the right training or tools, get them. If you want the company to pay, ask for it. If you're cold, wear a sweater to work. If the lighting is poor, buy a ten-dollar lamp. *Stop complaining and be accountable for yourself.*

This *employer* thinking approach distinguishes those willing to be accountable from the masses of those who are not. Rather than make an effort to understand how their actions affect the company's profitability—and their own well-being—employees with an *employee* mindset view their company as an ATM machine that coughs up a paycheck every couple of weeks after they complete a minimum number of tasks.

In contrast, employees with an *employer* mindset treat the team and business as though it's their own. They invest their discretionary effort, take account of their actions, and correct their own deficiencies instead of complaining about how the world's against them.

Defeatist, entitlement thinking is the bane of the modern workplace—and some say society at large. Who are you: someone who takes personal responsibility seriously, donning a can-do attitude like armor and fending for yourself? Or do you want to gripe and keep on failing to add value?

You don't accrue gripe time on your pay stub the way you do sick days. If you're a griper, you're just another expendable dime-a-dozen worker who's the first to get the boot when things go south.

You can think like an *employer* and build the company or think like an *employee* and punch the clock. Your choice.

OVERCOMING CONFLICT AND OTHER GROWING PAINS

Growth hurts—especially when it pulls you along faster than you'd like. You've explored how you have no choice but to change along with the business world, lest you and your team fall behind. This is an integral part of growth: bearing the pain even as it eats at you. Like a professional athlete, you don't ignore it; you simply find ways to handle it until you can fix it—and learn from the situation in the meantime.

The Painful Truth

Take personal criticism. Short of actually losing your job or suffering a demotion, getting criticized is probably one of the most painful workplace experiences possible.

But sometimes people need it. No matter where you stand in an organization, you can always improve your game. Many try to claim they're their own harshest critics, but that's rarely true. Even when it is, constructive criticism from someone you trust and respect matters more. Pain helps everyone learn and improve. Once you feel that pain, you can take measures to correct it.

You've probably received your share of criticism. I know I have! My audience members frequently complete evaluations after my talks, and I receive suggestions online weekly. Some comments I dismiss when they're obviously meant to be destructive; I consider the source and move on. But when people you respect take the time to explain what they perceive as your weaknesses, listen. They're trying to help you become a better person and a more skilled worker. If you have any doubts about what they've said, seek a second opinion from someone else you trust, someone who knows you well.

Practice these four tips for accepting and acting on constructive criticism:

1 LISTEN MORE, TALK LESS. Calmly absorb the criticism, being sure to think seriously about what the critic has said. Accept it gracefully; don't interrupt with excuses or denials, and never try to scapegoat someone else. Refuse to let your negative emotions get the better of you. Even painful feedback is useful, and you need it to improve your performance. Think back, and you'll realize your entire school career—from kindergarten on—was a constant back-and-forth session of criticism, feedback, and self-improvement.

2 ASK FOR SPECIFICS. If someone offers an offhand piece of vague criticism, don't dismiss it or obsess about what that person meant. Just ask for an example. If you think it might help, also ask for suggestions about what to do about it.

3 TAKE CORRECTIVE ACTION. Whether it involves signing up for an advanced English composition class or learning to use certain products, do whatever it takes to raise your skill set to the next level. Often your organization will help you with the cost; if it doesn't, do it on your own dime.

4 FOLLOW UP. You may need to speak to your critic again at some point to expand upon the original criticism and where you need to go from there. Take a deep breath and schedule a meeting. Once you've taken action to correct the problem, follow up again to determine whether your performance has improved in your critic's eyes. I particularly recommend this step if that person is your supervisor.

No Pain, No Gain

If life were always a bed of roses, we would never get up and try to improve ourselves. Sometimes you have to deal with the thorns. Ironically, the pain they cause will help you grow as a person. So listen and act on constructive criticism.

Even when you've fixed the problem, continue your improvement efforts. Eventually, you'll get so good at what you do that you'll never need to worry about that particular topic again—as long as you commit to maintaining high standards of performance. Then you can go on to the next thing you want to fix . . . because there will *always* be a next thing.

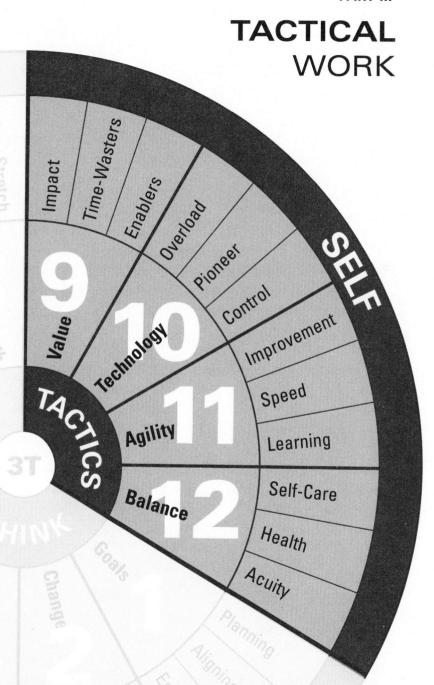

Truly successful executives are those who can thoroughly mine the intersection of efficiency and effectiveness to maximize their value and that of their team's—whether that team is a small group or an entire division, department, or organization.

Recall that effectiveness is doing the right things; efficiency is doing things right. The ores from which you smelt the alloy of both, doing the right things right, are the tactics by which you get things done and achieve strategic execution at the right time in the right place.

As a rule, you don't simply stumble across productivity— and it doesn't strike you out of the blue like a gift from Heaven. Purposeful productivity of the type you need boils down to four keys: Excellence, Planning, Effort, and Quality.

COMMITMENT TO EXCELLENCE

To achieve your goals requires nothing less than a commitment to do incredible work. Think of this attitude as leavening in a cake: without it, your team won't rise to the occasion. It's your responsibility to encourage team commitment to excellence in every way possible. Build an experienced, talented group, and then make each team member feel that visceral need to create a product or service that will carve out a large slice of the market share.

Typically, a commitment to excellence arises through factors such as these:

- Leadership by example

- A culture of mutual cooperation

- Motivation

- Employee empowerment

- Full engagement

INTELLIGENT PLANNING

Planning comprises the basic batter of your productivity cake, the body that gives the leavening something to act on. That means giving your folks enough time for their research, work, and strategic thinking. Look at what's going right (so you can continue it) and what's going wrong (so you can fix it). This leads to informed step-by-step planning, followed by goal setting and a point-by-point productivity plan. Do your deep thinking, set your milestones for each piece of the project, and only execute once you have enough information to do so—not a moment sooner or later.

FOCUSED EFFORT

Here's the heat that provides the energy and synergy that turns your goopy batter into a structured, final product. Your teammates will conduct the execution on the front lines; your primary job is to facilitate their progress and keep encouraging them. Clear away obstacles, elicit their advice, tap the knowledge of those outside the project, insert necessary changes with minimal disruption, block distractions, and keep an eye on the competition. Arrange the environment so your people can sink safely into the task at hand, becoming so focused they lose touch with the rest of reality for a short time.

INHERENT QUALITY

Once you've carefully selected, thoroughly mixed, and baked your productivity ingredients, a delicious result is inevitable. But remember: the final quality depends on you and your careful, heartfelt guidance. Some say cooks are only as good as their ingredients; I say cooks are only as good as their sense of purposeful productivity.

Remember, the balance of your tactical ingredients will vary according to the type of work you do. As Steve Gangwish, Vice President of CSS Farms, pointed out in our interview,

> We don't talk about working hours. . . . You just do whatever it takes to get the job done. When we do hire people from outside who don't know our culture, we're very open and honest about the time commitment of this job and what farming takes, and we definitely don't want to have any surprises there.

However you slice it, well-prepared tactical work guides, supports, and refines your final product: productivity. Like a catalyst in chemistry, it's not exactly a part of that product, but without it, the final result would not exist.

> **REMEMBER**
>
> The balance of your tactical ingredients will vary according to the type of work you do. However you slice it, well-prepared tactical work guides, supports, and refines your final product: productivity.

Impact

Time-Wasters

Enablers

TACTICAL WORK

9

VALUE

Focus on High-Impact Activities

How an executive does his or her personal work, and the milieu in which it occurs, is one of the most powerful aspects of managing that intersection of efficiency and effectiveness.

We know that time management determines how well we manage not only our own operational, day-to-day responsibilities, but that of our teams as well—and most of us do try to make sure we handle it in a manner that's both efficient and effective. But the blunt reality is that most leaders don't do it well.

Many of us waste more time than we should by trying to multitask and letting other people steal our attention a minute at a time. That's why we're wise to limit our activities to those that maximize productivity at the team level. But it all starts with your personal efforts.

THE IMPACT OF VALUING YOUR TIME

People say this so often that it's a cliché, and you're probably sick of hearing it. But I'm saying it anyway. *Time is your most precious resource.* We all get a finite amount, and once it's gone, there's no resupply. So you have to use what you have to maximize your impact.

Your best formula for both personal and team success is to make a serious effort to consistently value your time. Understand why your time matters as much as everyone else's, if not more, and how to conserve it in both personal and team ways.

One of the best ways to accomplish this is to tighten your self-discipline. As painful as it may seem in the moment, controlling nonproductive urges will ultimately get you where you want to be, often quicker than you expect. It may not be any fun, but it does get easier.

Time Well Spent

How you spend your time, of course, is constrained at least partly by the needs of your job. Steve Gangwish of CSS Farms told me he divides his time this way:

> I'd say I spend a third of my time talking to our team because we're remote. We're so spread out—a lot of times it's on the phone, sometimes in person. About a third of my time is [spent] talking with customers or vendors, third-party type folks. But a third of my time is [spent] on the road visiting our sites and doing operations. Whatever the question of the day is, or whatever the season, we're working on operational issues.

Microsoft's Chief Security Officer Mike Howard once spent about half his time on tactical work, but that figure has steadily dropped over the last decade or so. In an interview, he says,

> If I can look back twelve years ago, eight years ago, it's shifted radically. . . . I was spending half of my time on tactical issues—putting out fires, responding to this, that, and the other thing. A big piece of that obviously deals with talent. As you're vetting talent for a team, you obviously have to keep the ship running if you're the leader.
>
> So you're spending a fair amount of time actually responding to a crisis situation, if something blows up in the Middle East or Africa or Europe. And the higher-ups are going to be pinging you directly for any information. "Hey, we heard this happened in Paris," or "We heard this happened in Denmark, and what does this mean for us?"
>
> Over time, as you get the right talent and *they* manage those tactical things, and as the bosses become aware of the fact that you're informing them on a regular basis about what's going on, you become less inundated with the phone calls, the one-offs from bosses and higher-ups saying, "Hey, what about this? What about that?" They know we're taking care of it.
>
> It has shifted so radically that I spend probably maybe fifteen to twenty percent of my time on tactical issues. Maybe once or twice a week there is a fire that needs to be put out at my level. . . . But usually my leadership team can handle anything that I normally would have handled five, seven, eight years ago.

Promote the Professional Touch

True professionals know you have to do what you have to do, even when it's not pleasant or easy. They also know that to value and protect your time, you sometimes have to say *no* so you can reduce your workload to a realistic, productive level. No matter how eager to please you may be, killing yourself with overwork helps no one.

At the team level, this means you have to clear the way for your people to be equally as productive as you are. So make sure they understand what you want and need. Get acknowledgment from everyone in all directions. Productive communication will make sure your orders and requests are clear and understandable, thus saving time. Then you can climb onto your managerial bulldozer and act as the facilitator, removing any obstacles to your team's success.

The big goal is to save time for *everyone*. I firmly believe that too little work time is the biggest obstacle to doing productive work. So learn the art of the positive negative. That means when "don't" is the right choice, put it into effect. You have to know what *not* to do just as well as what you *must* do. This includes cutting the fat out of meetings, undeniably the most common time-waster executives deal with on a regular basis.

Time Management and Your Self-Worth

How much do you personally value your time? You may never have seriously considered the implications of that question, possibly because you don't really want to know. But to lead effectively, you have no choice but to address time-wasters and why they matter.

You're important to your organization; otherwise, you wouldn't hold the position you do. Therefore, your time must *also* matter a great deal. Don't assume your value is equivalent to your salary; the amount of money you earn is likely to be a lot less than the true worth you bring to the table. That's one reason your leaders value you. And as Microsoft's Mike Howard told me, "You cannot invest in yourself if you cannot manage your time properly, whether it's exercise or leadership or bettering yourself. . . . It all comes down to time management."

To do the best job possible, value your time both realistically and highly. Depending on your leadership position, your value to the organization may be thousands of dollars per hour. Once you've pinned down the value of your time, use these tips as you move forward:

1 **DELEGATE LIKE CRAZY.** Delegation is a basic tool of leadership, and your superiors expect you to use it. So delegate your authority and tasks as widely as possible, to capable people who can do certain things better than you can. Retain the few high-priority, high-value tasks only you can do most profitably. If your personal value is $1,000 an hour, don't waste time photocopying—the intern can do that for $10 an hour. It's your responsibility to match each duty to the best, most efficient team member for the price, or to outsource it if that makes better sense.

2 **AVOID FALSE ECONOMY.** If you go to a convention and pick a hotel a brisk fifteen-minute walk away from the convention center because it costs $75 per night instead of staying at the $125-per-night hotel hosting the convention, you've devalued your time. That half-hour spent walking back and forth may save your company $50 a day, but it costs the company $500 a day if you value your time at $1,000 an hour. That's really a loss of $450 per day.

If what you're doing costs more in terms of the value of your time than it's worth, stop doing it.

3 **ASSESS YOUR TEAM'S TIME VALUE AND MAKE CHANGES.** Have you ever thought about how much it costs some people to commute to work and back? If you have an employee with a long commute, consider allowing that person to telecommute. Let's say Sally lives an hour away from the office. She spends two hours in the car every day—about five hundred hours a year. Then there's the cost of gas. Assuming $15 per day for gas at 2015 prices, she spends about $3,750 annually (we won't even go into auto maintenance, oil, insurance, etc.). Now suppose she makes $25 per hour. If that's the basic value of her time, five hundred hours of commuting comes to $12,500. So far we're up to $16,250 (from her perspective) just for gas and time. Instead, let her telecommute so she can use those two hours productively, and renegotiate her hourly rate to reflect the new arrangement.

Think in Tradeoffs

Valuing your time and your team's requires considering the possible tradeoffs of everything you and they can do, from the structure of your work schedule to the best way to save money when traveling. Keep in mind that value constantly changes, so start thinking about and respecting your time in ways you've never done before.

Consider all the ways to improve your life and productivity from this single shift in perspective. Raise the value of your time, abandon false economy, and stop trying to do everything on the cheap.

CRACKING THE WHIP ON TIME-WASTERS

You've no doubt learned how to apply self-discipline, or you wouldn't have made it as far as you have in your career. Now apply that discipline to your team to ensure they aren't wasting valuable time either.

Clarify goals. Team goals will reflect your organizational goals, with some details specific to your crew. That doesn't mean everyone will know what to expect right off the bat. So when you first organize your team or when you add new people, spend face time with them to directly communicate the team goals and what you expect in their specific roles. Review those goals at regular intervals to maintain their clarity.

Rules matter. Clarify the organizational environment your team works in, explaining to team members precisely what you'll accept, what you won't, and what's explicitly against the rules. Detail the policies and standard operating procedures (SOP) regulating their actions. Once the SOPs and legal rules are understood, allow them to help shape the organizational environment.

Accountability is expected. Make it clear that, while you don't intend to be punitive (unless something goes badly wrong), you expect people to accept responsibility for everything they do, regardless of the outcome—yourself included. Honesty may be painful sometimes, but encourage your team members to come clean. How else can they learn?

Control boosts productivity. Self-control is crucial. Give your employees opportunities to improve their productivity by eliminating bad habits: overly long breaks, failure to take enough breaks, unproductive discussions, multitasking, procrastination, web surfing, and other time-wasters. Provide alternatives, and, if you must, let them know what to cut when they need to tighten up to be more productive.

Set a good example. If you make your own reputation and work habits assailable, your team members will follow your lead. If you show poor self-discipline, they'll be lax, too. So act as a role model and follow company policy. Don't expect the team to do what you say rather than what you do; the real world doesn't work that way.

Some leaders worry that having their people toe the line might trigger resentment and result in high turnover. Yes, it might, *if* you micromanage. But in my experience, workers expect and desire strong guidance. They respect tough-but-fair managers, especially when their management results in top marks and recognition from upper management, which can result in bonuses and promotions.

Firing Up the Managerial Bulldozer
As pointed out in chapter 5, leaders can no longer legislate strategic execution or plan too far into the future. Rigid strategies quickly become stale in the current business arena, and binding our front-line team members to them may result in failure. A more effective solution? Empower individuals to take ownership of their jobs so they can use whatever strategy works best in the moment to execute effectively and productively.

The truth is, leaders don't always know the best way to achieve a goal; they rely on their team members to tell them how. Today's leader functions best as a collaborative facilitator, asking questions and learning what obstacles lie in the way of success. They scout ahead and smooth the way for the team, so everyone can succeed more quickly.

A Broad Initiative

Here's how you can remove barriers to productivity:

1 **ELIMINATE TIME-WASTERS** by:
- Removing distractions.
- Walking around to understand what's happening.
- Clarifying priorities.
- Establishing a weekly interruption-free period.

2 **DELEGATE LOW-VALUE TASKS.** You have interns and entry-level employees especially for low-level tasks; if you don't, hire some. Don't let your people waste time on activities that belong to others.

3 **GRANT HIGHER LEVELS OF AUTHORITY.** Workflow should never slow or grind to a halt just because you have to give the okay to every little thing. Give people broad discretion to own their jobs and let them take action in a nonpunitive environment. That way, they can make the best decisions and get on with it. Often it's easier to beg forgiveness than get permission, especially when the supervisor isn't available.

Microsoft's Mike Howard advises,

> Part of continuous improvement is allowing people to make mistakes. If they make [the same mistake] twice, that's a problem. Allowing people to make mistakes and not killing them over it is important, while encouraging them by saying, "Okay, you can learn from this," and "How do you learn from this so it won't happen again?"

Colin Powell always said, "When troops stop

bringing me problems, that's when we've got a leadership issue." You want them to be comfortable with bringing problems to you, knowing that even if it's something bad, you will work through it. I'd rather have them bring it to me than try to fix something they can't fix on their own, and then it gets worse.

4 **INTERCEPT THE RED TAPE.** Deal with the bureaucracy or politics yourself, so your team won't have to. When you can't, work toward streamlining bureaucratic requirements so you won't have to deal with so many workflow bottlenecks.

Obstacles Aplenty

In any organization, scores of obstacles will gouge potholes in your team's path or plop boulders in their way. Those obstacles may be bureaucratic, technological, procedural, or artifacts of old ways of thinking. In the old days, maybe it was acceptable to let your people thread their way through that minefield on their own. But you can no longer spare the time. Fire up the procedural machine and put the hammer down, filling in the potholes and pushing those boulders out of the way so your team can follow with ease.

Think of yourself as Daniel Boone with a bulldozer. Now *that's* trailblazing.

ENABLERS TO HELP OTHERS SAVE TIME

Every second you or your team members save goes toward increased productivity. Sometimes, knowing what *not* to do is the best thing for you—though this fact can become difficult to recognize if you focus so tightly on what you can do strategically that you miss the obvious choices regarding what *not* to do.

Short, Sweet, and to the Point

Not only do you have to say no to yourself when dealing with unprofitable tasks but sometimes you also have to say no to your coworkers, even your supervisor. And when you do, you have to mean it.

In a corporate environment where a can-do, go-team attitude is important for success, you may think you should say yes to every task thrust at you. Sometimes it seems impossible to say no. If your manager drops another project on your plate while you're running out the door, or an end user asks if you can add just *one* more little feature while you're elbow-deep in the code, it's challenging to refuse.

But while it may make you feel anxious to say no, sometimes you have no choice but to refuse requests—or demands—to avoid drowning in overwork. After all, a physical or emotional breakdown would be bad for your productivity. Even if you've never broken down, you've seen it happen to others, and you've probably felt the strain when you're weighed down by enough straws to almost break your back. Feeling overstressed can happen to anyone with responsibility who juggles multiple projects.

When you're on the ragged edge of taking a hammer to your computer, something's gotta give. If you learn to say no to people just a *little* more often, it won't be you doing the hammering.

Revenge of the Yes-Man

Years ago, I saw a *Wizard of Id* comic strip that made me laugh. It showed a man in courtier's attire running over the landscape, shouting "No! No! No! No!" When one soldier asked another, "What's with him?" his buddy replied, "That's the king's Yes-Man. It's his day off."

Like that Yes-Man or Yes-Woman, you have to say no at times, because things will keep coming at you until you wave the white flag. Overcommitting to work will tangle you up so badly that your performance will suffer. So when one of your coworkers asks if you can do just *one* little favor, check your schedule. If you don't have enough time, tell that person you just can't take it on right now. Don't be snappy about it; just don't take everything people try to hand you.

And don't put everyone else's needs ahead of your own. Don't "volunteer" to coach the company's softball team, or bake a cake for someone's birthday, or do a quick analysis for the guy in the next cube—no matter how much someone pressures you. The one exception? If that person already has your manager's backing, and you can't validly challenge the request. You only have so much time in any particular work-week and there's no way to add more, so don't let someone else overdraw your account.

Here are three creative ways to say no:

1 **OFFER TO MEET PEOPLE HALFWAY.** Unless the item is higher value than what's on your plate and has your manager's blessing, tell them, "I can't handle this now, but if it can wait two weeks, I can look at it then." If it's time-sensitive, you're off the hook. If not, it can wait until a slot opens in your schedule. Or your coworker may magically find someone else who can do it now. You can also make an introduction. Say, "While this isn't a good fit for me right now, here's someone who might be able to help," or "These resources might help you find what you're looking for," and direct your coworker accordingly.

2 **ASK IF YOU CAN GET STARTED NOW AND FINISH LATER.**
If you can do a certain amount of the task but can't do it all, offer to do what you can. The person might be able to find someone else to do the rest.

3 **PUNT IT.** If others ask for your help with a task and you can't or don't want to give it, ask them to make the request through your manager. They may be reluctant to do so, and, even if they do, your manager might shoot them down. My friends' assistants often ask my office manager to show them how to do something or train them, and she always copies me in, so I can say, "Her time is fully committed supporting our business, so I regret we won't be able to do that for you."

What If It's Your Boss?

If your direct superior keeps putting more projects onto your already overloaded plate, you'll need help prioritizing. Find out the ranking of the tasks in terms of importance and give your manager your estimated dates of completion. When asked, some managers will reply with a less-than-useful, "Everything's top priority." In other words, *nothing* is. Discuss a priority framework to guide you, so you make sure to accomplish the top priorities first.

Others may want you to do everything ASAP. Not useful. If this is the response, you'll just have to say, "I'll work on Project A first, then . . ." If you get an objection, ask what you should do instead. Point out you can only do one thing at a time effectively and ask for help prioritizing. There's no way you can complete five significant projects all due Friday without something breaking down.

Even when you believe you can't say no, find a way to do

it anyway. Your productivity and sanity will thank you. And recognize the value of this technique when your team members apply it to you, too.

Put Your Foot Down

It doesn't matter what people do in their free time as long as it's legal. But in almost every case, that right ends at the office door.

Furthermore, doing anything morally off-base delays the achievement of an organization's strategic goals, and the gnashing of teeth that ensues from such behavior wastes valuable time. While team members are in your domain, make sure they put on their teamwork hats, leaving personal opinion, prejudices, and negativity behind until they go home. At the same time, be careful if you're conducting professional interactions on your personal time. Remind them:

1 **DON'T GOSSIP.** People are social beings who tend to spread news about others, especially if it seems juicy. Don't. So what if someone's marriage is in trouble or if so-and-so has no sense of style? Silly gossip wastes time, while making you and your team look bad. It may damage the reputation of those involved. For example, a colleague recently had the displeasure of watching a family member's small business erode because of vicious lies spread by a former employee.

2 **DON'T LET ANYONE DUCK RESPONSIBILITY.** Accountability offers a touchstone for both integrity and success. Urge your people to admit when they've done something wrong, or when something they tried didn't work. Despite the example set in corporate scandals during recent years,

finger-pointing, scapegoating, and ducking responsibility all damage trust and inevitably degrade the team. Accept your errors, take your licks, and move on.

3 **AVOID DEFEATIST THINKING.** Sometimes a team needs a devil's advocate to help them move forward along the most appropriate path. But once the team or team leader has made a decision, team members must accept it and go on, not whine about how the decision is unfair and will never work. Being a "PITA negatron," as one colleague calls it (I'll let you figure out what the acronym stands for) won't win you friends and will inevitably slow workflow.

Enable More Productive Meetings

As you can likely attest, most business meetings waste productive time and last far longer than they should. But until humans learn to communicate telepathically, meetings will remain a necessary evil—not only as a means of exchanging ideas and information but also as a way of building relationships with others.

You might not like them, but you can certainly make them more tolerable by applying these tips:

1 **DECIDE IF THE MEETING IS EVEN NECESSARY.** Can you handle the issue with a few emails or a conference call? If so, do it. Why call a full meeting if you don't need one?

2 **START ON TIME.** If people don't arrive on time, tough. Start when you agreed to, and don't start over just because individuals arrive late. Latecomers can check the minutes later to find out what you discussed before they arrived, or they can get notes from a colleague.

3 **USE A FACILITATOR.** Have someone direct the meeting. That person's role should include keeping the discussion on topic, acknowledging speakers, soliciting opinions from quieter attendees, and keeping a few people from dominating the meeting. They should also end the meeting on time. This will go easier if you make the agenda crystal clear well in advance. People need to know why they're meeting and what you expect to accomplish as a result. Distribute the agenda and associated materials at least twenty-four hours in advance. Be clear at the end about what decisions were made, as well as who's responsible for what and by when.

4 **LIMIT ATTENDEES.** If a meeting has little to do with particular people, don't invite them. "Showing the flag" isn't a good enough reason to have someone at a meeting. Send those who don't attend a copy of the minutes if they need to have a general idea of what happened. It's cheaper and simpler. The same goes for you attending other people's meetings. Mike Howard at Microsoft puts it this way: "I don't take meetings unless I need to make a decision or if my boss is calling for me to be there. . . . If I'm just going to sit there like a bump on a log, I've got better things to do."

While business meetings may never be a blast, you *can* make them effective and efficient if you implement the points suggested here.

10

TECHNOLOGY

Master Data Handling and Workflow

How executives organize their personal work matters more now than it ever has. Things as simple as efficient time management, organization, and email processing help you save time and sharpen the knife of effectiveness. Do you know how to triage your time, abandoning and delegating tasks until all that remains is the lean, profitable meat of your job? Even something as simple as how you handle information can smooth your workflow, saving you more of that most precious of resources: time.

Technology has been a blessing in this regard, but it's a two-edged sword. On the one hand, it's helped make modern workers more productive. The cloud computing phenomenon alone has simplified access to anywhere/anytime information, letting us do our work no matter where we are.

Conversely, technology can be tyrannical. Not only do you

risk *Schlimmbesserung* (the effort to make something better that actually makes it worse; in this case, the flood of new work triggered by supposed timesaving inventions), it sometimes makes it easier for others to steal proprietary information. You may also become trapped by your technology, unable to survive without it.

REINING IN INFORMATION OVERLOAD

Triage is a medical term, but it applies well to business situations. Basically, the idea is to continually reorganize tasks by priority, so the most important or most pressing ones come first. On the battlefield, medics triage by the severity of the wound; the most life-threatening injuries and burn victims are shuffled to the top of the list. The triage order may change moment by moment. Part of the process is making sure those least likely to survive are made as comfortable as possible but placed at the bottom of the triage list. That last bit may sound brutal, but medics have to do it in order to save as many lives as possible.

To smooth your workflow and make the best use of your time, you have to adapt a triage mentality for yourself and your team. Even in the best of times, you'll find that some of your tasks and projects are dying, and that it's past time to save them or make them worthwhile—so you have to let them go.

Everything that grows must be pruned. With plants, that may be literal; with animals and people, less so. We remove excess hair, cut our nails, and lose dead skin cells naturally as we go about our lives (sometimes with a little help from a loofah sponge). Our brains automatically prune connections between brain cells so we're not overwhelmed with sensation or thought. Similarly, we have to prune our ideas and our schedules to function more effectively.

So get busy with your scalpel and cut out the nonurgent. Trim away anything that doesn't contribute to strategic execution. Too often, we waste time on activities that don't align with corporate priorities, either from efforts to try new things or because we're still using legacy processes we should have tossed years ago.

Take a look at what you're doing that might be detracting from your productivity and eliminate the least useful items. Push the triage process hard and fast, and you'll get it done.

One critical area you'll have to triage is your information inflow. The average person is inundated with information, in the form of news, educational studies, advertisements, casual entertainment, the Internet, email, and more. Don't drown in it. When you triage that as well, you can save an enormous amount of time.

Social researcher Richard Saul Wurman once calculated that every issue of the *New York Times* contained more information than the average person in Elizabethan England learned in his or her lifetime.[36] Wurman published that observation back in 1987—before the information explosion we call the Internet got started. Imagine how much worse it is today. Add in easy access to nearly every book, magazine, and newspaper ever published, and it's hardly surprising that, according to research analyst Jonathan B. Spira, "94% of knowledge workers have felt overwhelmed to the point of incapacitation by the amount of information they encounter on a daily basis."[37]

There are tens of millions of information workers in the United States alone. The fact that 94 percent of us have been vapor-locked by information overload at one time or another has sobering ramifications for productivity.

Reducing Your Information Intake

The only way to overcome "infobesity" is to triage mercilessly, then reduce the amount you take in forever. Keep these
tips in mind as you work toward stemming the info-tide.

1 **LIMIT YOUR EXPOSURE TO EXTERNAL INFORMATION
AT WORK.** Instead of checking social media during your
lunch and breaks, actually take those breaks. Eat, talk to
people, go for a walk—just get away from your desk. You
have enough work-related information to deal with. When
you *do* check the news, don't let links and ads drag you off in
unproductive directions.

2 **CHECK YOUR EMAIL AS LITTLE AS POSSIBLE.** Focus
on email several discrete times a day, rather than keeping your inbox open and constantly monitoring it. I process
email five to seven times a day, getting the inbox down
to zero (using Outlook's "Move to Tasks" functionality),
reprioritizing accordingly, and then working for a focused
period. During that period, I don't check email, I turn my
smartphone to airplane mode, and forward my calls to
voicemail. Mike Howard of Microsoft has a similar process.
"I check in three times a day, which equates to an hour
and a half max of doing email."

Setting email filters also helps. Every email client lets
you filter email according to specific rules, automatically
discarding messages that fail to meet the standards you set.
Blacklists tell the system to discard email messages from
specific addresses, so you never even see them. Whitelists
specify precisely who you're willing to receive mail from, accepting only their emails and blocking the rest. You can also
create rules to automatically file messages with certain words

in the subject line in particular folders, or to play a sound when you receive an email from a particular person.

3 **EMPLOY THE RIGHT MEANS OF COMMUNICATION.** Sometimes it's more efficient to pick up the phone rather than continue an email volley. In other cases, nothing beats a face-to-face meeting. Rather than waste time and increase unnecessary information, carefully select the most efficient means of communication for each issue.

4 **HONE YOUR ONLINE RESEARCH SKILLS.** Take advantage of Boolean data type operators online and other simple shortcuts to streamline info-searches and return fewer, better-targeted results.

5 **MAXIMIZE READING TIME.** If you have a lot of material to wade through, adopt a speed-reading system such as J. Michael Bennett's rhythmic perusal method. Carry around material for downtime reading as printouts in your briefcase, PDFs on your iPad, or ebooks on your Kindle. That way, you can catch up whenever you're stuck in traffic, standing in line, or waiting in the doctor's office.

Grabbing a Lifeline

If you ever find yourself paralyzed by information overload, scale back as far as you possibly can. Ideally, you'll end up well below your overwhelm threshold. Then you can start adding back information sources one at a time, gradually refining your ability to handle each until you feel you can add another. Maintain the methods I've outlined here, and you'll find it easier to handle the inflow in the future.

THE 6-D INFORMATION MANAGEMENT SYSTEM™

Six Basic Decisions
and Equivalent Action Steps

1 **DISCARD.** Get rid of as much as possible at the very beginning. Unless you have a good reason to keep it, delete it.

2 **DELEGATE.** You may be able to forward the email to someone else (or Assign a Task in Outlook). The goal here is to get it under someone else's control if possible.

3 **DO.** This works when an item requires your personal action, and you can handle it right then. Choose this option if you can reply to the message in less than three minutes.

4 **DATE.** If you can't do it now but still have to do it, turn it into a task (click the Move button and select Tasks) to activate it into your time management system, so it appears again on the right Start Date.

5 **DRAWER.** File it or digitize it for future reference. In this case, you don't need to do anything, but you can't just throw it away; it may come in handy later.

6 **DETER.** Stop receiving the information, by taking steps such as unsubscribing to newsletters or using Rules to direct reports to folders. Just make sure it stops coming to you for good.

The 6-D Information Management System™

I first introduced my 6-D Information Management System in *Leave the Office Earlier* (see facing chart). I've taught it consistently since the 1990s, because you don't abandon what works. It's been the subject of lots of "the sincerest form of flattery," but the original derives from six decisions that all begin with the letter "D"—hence the name.

You can use the 6-D System to process and fine-tune *any* type of information. Nowadays we focus mainly on email, but these steps apply to paperwork and voicemail as well.

If the instructions in the facing chart are Greek to you, visit www.TheProductivityPro.com/outlook for details about my twelve-hour video tutorial on using Microsoft Outlook effectively and efficiently.

PIONEER NEW TECHNOLOGY

Gene Roddenberry, the creator of *Star Trek*, once explained its appeal as "technology unchained." In the *Star Trek* universe, technology has become so advanced that poverty (and money) no longer exists, and doctors can cure most illnesses. That doesn't mean Starfleet doesn't run afoul of Klingons or the Borg occasionally, however. And sometimes technology backfires in unexpected ways. The same thing can happen to you in the here-and-now.

New technology can have its dangers, especially in the workplace. Improperly implemented, it can slow or stop productivity. Additionally, inexperienced or malicious users can leave backdoors open for hackers and identity thieves to waltz right in and steal or corrupt data. So before you dive in, dip a toe in the waters first.

Here are four suggestions to keep in mind before you take the plunge with new technology:

1 STUDY ITS IMPACT. Will the new technology really upgrade productivity? If not, why bother? If so, could it still be more trouble than it's worth? Is the new functionality worth the cost of the training you'll have to pay for when you upgrade? How will the new technology help or hinder you? Large organizations sometimes skip versions of Microsoft Outlook, for example. Many chose to go directly from 2007 to 2013, skipping the 2010 version, because 2013's functionality didn't change much from 2010's, and upgrading thousands of users is both expensive and complicated. Examine the pros and cons in detail before you implement. If the cons outweigh the pros, forget it.

2 CALCULATE THE COSTS. At some point, you'll have no choice but to upgrade. Either manufacturers will stop supporting your old tech, or everyone else will adopt the new version, leaving you in the dust. But ask yourself: must you do it *now*? You may want to wait until the price drops and the bugs are fixed. In 1993, dual-core 486 IBM clones were the acme of modern desktop computing. Within a year, manufacturers couldn't give them away because everyone wanted Pentiums.

3 CONSIDER *SCHLIMMBESSERUNG*. Will the upgrade increase your productivity over the long run—or will you end up working harder and longer? The German word *Schlimmbesserung* is particularly apt for "time-saving" technology that actually creates more work. Before the invention of the vacuum cleaner, most floors were made of easily swept hardwood or tile. Carpets were few, small, and ornamental, and got a good cleaning a few times a year. Afterward, wall-to-wall carpeting became popular, and homemakers found themselves vacuuming several times a week—a classic example of *Schlimmbesserung*.

4 **INCLUDE AN EXIT STRATEGY.** Ease into the change. Test the new technology to make sure it does all it promises—and don't hesitate to roll back to your old tech if it doesn't. Back in 2001, a telephony company that's now part of Tektronix Communications implemented a company-wide computer upgrade that the IT department promised would help everyone do their jobs better. They were well into it before many employees realized they'd actually lost functionality. Vital software wouldn't run on the new operating system (OS), and often the new OS wouldn't run on the computers, because the computers themselves were outdated. By then, the IT team had already purchased hundreds of expensive OS licenses and had committed to the changeover. Because decent workstations cost more than $2,000 back then, it cost quite a bit more than expected to upgrade and replace the systems of all 250-plus employees.

Handle with Care

We realize new technology can be dangerous when misused, but we use it anyway. Why? Because the benefits usually outweigh the dangers.

This has been especially true of the electronic technology that's recently revolutionized the white-collar workplace. As long as you take reasonable care when adopting new technology, the worst it will do is slow you down a bit before you retrain, regroup, and recharge.

Get Your Head into the Clouds

Speaking of revolutionary technology: not so long ago, the ability to access our data anywhere at any time would have seemed miraculous. But after near-ubiquitous Wi-Fi laid the foundation, cloud computing took it from there. These days, smart companies have made "the cloud" a mainstay of their productivity and data security plans.

Despite the name, your data's not really floating around in the air like water vapor. It's in vast data warehouses, often located in remote venues packed full of humming data servers. That's not so different from the data farms of yore, but the strength of the cloud concept lies in its structure. The system backs up cloud data in multiple locations so it can be restored easily.

The productivity benefits are obvious. Not only is cloud storage free or cheap, but also you're no longer chained to one location or device. If you're stuck waiting for a delayed flight, you can turn on your smartphone's wireless hotspot and go to work on your laptop or tablet. If you're giving a speech and your laptop decides to die on you in the hotel, your presentation isn't in danger if you housed your files on the cloud through such services as Google Drive or Dropbox.

You can be on the other side of the world on business and easily grab files; indeed, most developed nations have pulled ahead of the United States in implementing cloud computing. Google Docs, Dropbox, Evernote, MS OneDrive, Hightail, the Amazon Web Services, and many other cloud services have made it a piece of cake to transfer and share files, back up data, sync between devices, and ensure you can access it all wherever you find yourself.

The security benefits are exceptional as well. You no longer need to worry about a single regional event—such as a huge blackout—blocking access to or killing your data; cloud storage is decentralized. The integrity of the data is on a good footing, too, because there's no single server that hackers can loot to steal all the data—though occasional breaches do occur.

CONTROL YOUR TECHNO-TOOLS

Ideally, the only purpose of a tool is to gain and leverage an advantage. But often this comes with a price. The mobility offered by automobiles comes at the price of gasoline, maintenance, and insurance costs, for example. Sometimes a tool is just too easy to use, so we use it for everything, blurring the line between work and personal applications.

Modern information technology is a prime example of the latter. Consider the time we spend surfing the Internet, responding to social media, tapping out text messages, reading and replying to email—all things originally intended to improve our productivity. Mostly they have, but some people become so focused on these that the tools run their lives.

At first glance, this may seem ludicrous—but have you ever loitered around the house waiting for an important phone call, felt lost without your smartphone, or stressed out if your email was down?

If so, keep these tips in mind when dealing with workplace info-tech:

1 **KNOW WHEN TO TUNE OUT AND TURN OFF.** When it's time to be off work, *be off work*. Power down and live in the moment with family and friends, or you'll never learn to set firm boundaries between personal and work time. You need your time off to recharge. Crunch times, when you absolutely have to focus to finish something on schedule, also represent good times to turn away from distracting technology and do your work the old-fashioned way.

Be especially sure to turn off your alerts. Unless you work in social media or online customer service, you don't need to know the instant every email pops into your mailbox, and you certainly don't need Twitter to tell you someone just mentioned you in a tweet. Even a minor distraction—like stopping to read an email—can destroy your focus, and it takes several minutes to get back on track.

2 **LIMIT YOUR INTERNET USAGE.** Internet-blocking software can keep you honest, so you don't pop over to ESPN and check the box scores when you should be poring over your team's monthly metrics. Programs like Freedom and Net Nanny can help you break the habit by limiting access for certain sites to specific times of the day.

3 **TAKE A TECHNOLOGY SABBATICAL.** If you can get away with it, cut off an offending technology altogether for a while or make yourself available only at certain times. You might feel anxious the first couple of days, but you'll settle into it. Taking a break proves you're still in control.

4 **STOP THE ALERTS.** While I love my smartphone, some folks never seem to put theirs down. Not only is a good smartphone a telephone, it's a personal digital assistant, a camera, a gaming platform, an email terminal, a texting device, a computer, and a TV. In many ways, a smartphone's organizer aspects—especially calendaring and contact data— make these tech toys invaluable. If you find yourself addicted, though, turn off your notifications and alerts and put the phone on airplane mode while you focus on a project.

Even the most useful tool can become an enemy when it distracts you from your work, however subtly. Your best bet? Exercise iron discipline, simply refusing to use your tools in ways you never intended. Tools, no matter how high-tech, are made for *you* to use. Don't let them take over your life and keep you from spending nontech time with your loved ones.

Social Media Landmines

Even something as simple as posting to Facebook or Twitter can hurt you. Every hiring manager has a story about someone who botched a job interview or torpedoed a career due to thoughtless use of social media sites. I know someone whose close friend lost his job after making negative comments about his company's investment prospects on MySpace (remember that site?).

Few people think twice about posting party pictures on their Facebook pages or casual trash talk on Twitter. But your prospective employer or current company also has an online presence, and they may keep an eye on you—which isn't tough when you voluntarily post content for the world to see. As your mother taught you, if you can't say something nice, don't say anything at all.

As painful as accidentally harpooning yourself with an ill-judged post may be, wasting time is the real danger here, because it damages productivity. Even otherwise savvy social media users can fall prey to this problem. I use social media for professional reasons, and you may do so as well if, say, you're a marketing exec, an HR manager recruiting people to your company, an entrepreneur reaching out to prospects, a job seeker networking for a new position, or a professional simply staying in touch with customers.

However, many business uses of social media aren't work-related at all. The traditional work year clocks in at 2,080 hours, which is 260 work days annually. Suppose you spend only 10 minutes each workday tweeting or checking Facebook when you should be working. That comes to 2,600 minutes a year—the equivalent of 43 work hours—down the drain! If your manager deducted that at the end of the year, you'd have a week less paid time off.

Unless social media provides part of your income or your job requires you to monitor it, then it has a lousy return on investment. Even if you use it sensibly at work, it may *still* have a poor ROI. Do you *know* if the time you spend on social media yields high results?

You'd kick anything else with a bad ROI to the curb, so if your social media activities aren't providing results, tune out, drop out, and refocus on what matters. Save Facebook, Twitter, and Instagram for your nonwork time. Even then, take care what you post—because everyone's on the Internet nowadays.

11
AGILITY
Maximize Speed and Flexibility

Strength in the post–Great Recession environment is based on agility. Effective, efficient execution demands it. Agility means responding to change of any kind with speed and flexibility, whether it's a new client demand or a paradigm shift. Handling new challenges on the fly, swerving onto a new course, stopping suddenly, and reversing direction—it's all in a day's work for the modern business professional.

The theme of flexibility has run through this entire book: triage tasks, embrace change, avoid techno-traps, improve continually, and facilitate tasks, to name just a few.

All that really matters in terms of productivity are results—another of this book's primary themes. It doesn't matter how many hours you put in or how many to-do tasks you scratch off your list; what matters is whether you've produced at a high level or not. No one can afford to just serve time until the end of the day, or the end of a career. Nor can you allow paralysis or procrastination to slow you down.

As Darren Smith of John Hancock Investments noted in our interview,

> The velocity of change in business is constantly acceler-
> ating, so in order to remain competitive, it is critical to
> stay agile. The landscape is littered with examples of com-
> panies like Blackberry and Sears that were once dominant
> franchises that didn't stay flexible and lost their edge. So,
> agility and flexibility are more crucial than ever.
>
> However, a company must also have a clear corporate
> vision, definite strategic objectives, and very clear operat-
> ing priorities that form a solid foundation for success. If
> this structure is in place and is adhered to, then necessary
> adjustments can be made as business conditions change,
> but it doesn't derail the company or undermine the firm's
> strategic plan.

Speed and flexibility are especially important at a team level. Crisis requires a tight focus on the need of the hour and a rapid response time.

IMPROVEMENT: WORKING HARD ON THE RIGHT THINGS

If you're having trouble determining whether your team is productive or just busy, assume the latter. Productivity should be glaringly obvious. But if any doubts linger, consider these points:

- *How measurable are your goals?* Everything you do should contribute to something profitable. Clarify your goals with your team if they're confused about priorities.

If you can't tell how an activity moves you toward your goals, then it's suspect and may be ripe for elimination. Always track results with easily readable metrics.

- *How's your ROI?* Does your team's output consistently earn the organization more than it pays you? If not, start honing ROI. Outsource tasks that people outside your team can do better and cheaper. Stop doing tasks below your pay grade, and don't micromanage. Always look for a more profitable alternative to every task.

- *Is your meeting meter running?* As you rise in leadership, you'll be spending more time in meetings, because they represent your work—decision-making. But they can steal your time if you're not careful. If a meeting doesn't come with a purpose, an agenda, and decisions to be made, skip it. Leave at the promised end time. Encourage others to be brief and stick to the point with their comments.

- *Are you proactive or reactive?* Do you and your team leap into action only when prodded, or do you review your strategy on a regular basis so you greet change with enthusiasm and aplomb?

My friend Randy Pennington puts it aptly in his book title, *Results Rule!*, and he's right. It boils down to this: productive teams produce results; busy teams produce busywork. Unless you work for an organization such as an international charity in which results aren't immediately apparent, it shouldn't take you more than five minutes to determine if your team is being productive.

Leveraging Agility

Given today's go-go-go approach to modern business, agility is applicable to most fields. Software development already has its model of Agile Project Management (APM), which doesn't rely on the classic "waterfall" model of sequential project management, where one stage can't proceed without results from the preceding stage. The obvious problem with the waterfall model is that if only one stage of a workflow cascade dams up, everyone down the line stalls out until someone clears the blockage. This is expensive and wasteful, and most of us have experienced it.

A more flexible model breaks a project into manageable pieces, all with independent milestones, due dates, and testing phases that team members can handle independently if necessary. That way, when a delay occurs in one area, it doesn't stop the entire project dead in its tracks. Take these actions the next time you assign your team a new project:

1 **EXAMINE IT CAREFULLY FROM ALL ANGLES.** Focus on the needs and requirements first. Think about where and how you can split the project into discrete pieces that particular team members or subteams can handle. Film crews have used a piecemeal process for decades. They will shoot unrelated scenes back-to-back based on factors like weather, actor availability, lighting, access to a location, etc. Often, one unit shoots one set of scenes as a second shoots another.

2 **CUT THE DIAMOND.** You can easily "part out" some projects, but you will have to deal with others more carefully, much like cutting a diamond. Once you've determined you can split the project into pieces, do so. Take your chisel and tap it carefully with the hammer to break the proj-

ect up. Hand the pieces out to the people best suited for them, complete with their own specific milestones and deadlines.

3 **BUILD IN FLEXIBILITY.** There's a reason your skeleton consists of many pieces that can bend and stretch in several directions. Your bones could be a lot stronger if your arms, legs, spine, and the like were all single pieces, but if that were the case, you'd sacrifice all flexibility and agility— and that's just not acceptable. Plus, if one bone breaks, it doesn't render your entire body useless.

A project built from many independent parts is naturally more flexible than a sequential "waterfall" project. It more easily absorbs the need for changes, additional testing, and new features as they arise. You can also implement feed-back more quickly. As Janie Wade, Senior Vice President of Finance for Baylor Scott & White Health, points out in an interview,

> Even though we plan, we know unexpected opportunities will come our way. We allow flexibility in our planning to take advantage of these opportunities. We might have to push another project out a year if we determine that we don't have enough time or resources to execute both strategies simultaneously or if we think too many initiatives at once will negatively affect front line staff. Front line staff care for patients. We want them to be able to focus on that.

4 **PUT IT BACK TOGETHER.** As sections of the project come in, slide them in place, leaving space for the later bits to allow greater flexibility in terms of responding to customer and market needs. This requires careful planning and preparation, perhaps more so than traditional project

management. Yet, it not only saves time overall but also facilitates decision-making and eliminates waste. You don't have to wait until the end to cut out what doesn't work and graft in better concepts and newer features.

You can learn a lot from software designers and film crews about the agile approach you need to not only succeed but also blow people away—and you don't have to sacrifice a speck of quality to do it.

No One Should Be Indispensable
If you want your team, division, department, or company to truly improve, you have to hire for versatility, not indispensability. If someone is indispensable, then you can't replace them. If you can't replace them, the team can't advance without them. So if that person dies, leaves, or even takes a vacation and forgets to leave the keys to the filing cabinet (metaphorically speaking), the team is unable to move forward.

No one on your team should be indispensable. Ever. Not even you—or your company can never promote you. Would you want a car with irreplaceable parts? Of course not; eventually it would break down, and you could never fix it. The same holds true for a business team.

Instead, make sure your teammates are somewhat interchangeable, so you can maintain your productivity no matter what.

Building in Backup
Keep these four strategies in mind:

1 **HIRE FOR REDUNDANCY.** While you may not need two writers or three coders for your new video game, it's still a good idea to hire people with a range of skills that overlap, just in case. As you build your team, look for people who can act as pinch hitters when necessary or those you can groom to take over another position in the future.

2 CROSS-TRAIN. To maintain the integrity of the team, send members to classes so they can better understand what their teammates do. Host brown-bag luncheons where one person explains the details of his or her job, or have one team member "shadow" another to learn that person's duties. Make the training appropriate to their positions; your support staff may not need to master the latest programming languages, but your programmers certainly do.

3 DOCUMENT EVERYTHING. Record each task each person on your team does in plain English, complete with graphics, so anyone with basic knowledge of the discipline can pick up the manual and roll with it. No one does this better than McDonald's, which is why the company can quickly train inexperienced teenagers to produce a consistent product worldwide.

4 PLAN FOR THE FUTURE. Someday, you'll retire or move up; you may even leave for another company. Therefore, you'll need to groom a successor to handle your duties, either when you leave or when you can't be at work due to illness, travel, or vacation. The same goes for your senior team members. Succession planning is a basic duty of all organizations. Hire with succession in mind. When we nominate new board members of the National Speakers Association, we always ask, "Can we see this person becoming president of NSA someday?" If you don't handle hiring personally, impress your precise needs upon your HR reps.

Once you've chosen a successor for a position, start providing the training needed to move that person up as circumstances require.

Up or Out

It may *sound* good to be indispensable or irreplaceable—but don't you believe it. The truly indispensable person is stuck, and heaven help their team if something happens to them or they quit.

Rather than let anyone become indispensable, make sure everyone is replaceable. That way, you can safeguard team productivity while rewarding individual competence and initiative.

SPEED TO THE NEED OF THE HOUR

One aspect of flexibility leaders often overlook is that their management style has to change according to the situation or person. For example, you may have to be more stringent during crunch time to complete a project on time and within budget, but that need only be temporary before you return to your normal laid-back self. You also have to understand how to handle individual team members—and know when they need a manager as opposed to a coach, or vice versa.

That means cluing in to the differences between managing and coaching, while knowing when each is called for.

Despite what some people may think, business leadership is no walk in the park. I can tell you from personal experience—and from the testimony of plenty of clients—that the combination of mental work, social interaction, project juggling, time management challenges, high pressure, responsibility, and variability makes it one of the most demanding types of work anyone can take on. The hours are long and the stress inevitable.

But if organizations expect to accomplish anything of consequence, they must have managers. While managers may not *directly* produce what an organization makes, they facilitate and organize team productivity, which clears the way for others to succeed.

Yet a true leader is more than a manager driving the team's performance. He or she acts as a coach in the best sense of the word, laying out the general strategy with talented, trusted team members who then run with the ball while the coach steps out of the way.

So when should you be one or the other—a manager versus a coach?

The Managerial Side of the Job

Managers often have to tell others what to do. You may have to act from greater experience, knowledge, or training, directly passing on your requirements to your team through tasking, directives, and initiatives. This most often occurs in situations where immediate needs are paramount, and you need to achieve specific outcomes quickly. Your team looks to you for answers—and rightly so. You want them to think for themselves, but sometimes a team needs someone to coordinate all the pieces of the project.

As a pure manager, you direct from a position of authority while guiding your team toward a specific outcome. Situations where you need to manage include:

- Dealing with crises that require fast results.
- Handling inexperienced personnel, especially those tackling a task for the first time.
- Making sure your team completes a low-level or unpopular task.
- Meeting difficult deadlines when every minute counts.

These situations require quick, decisive action focused on high productivity and achievement.

The Flipside: Coaching

In this era of independent thinkers who must often execute instantly without awaiting permission, the leader's job has expanded. No longer does a leader just tell people what to do: a leader guides their team in their work, clears obstacles from their paths, and supports their immediate and long-term career goals.

Trusted, experienced, and efficient personnel form the hub of the true wheel of productivity, so coaching skills should take the lion's share of your time. Coaching works best in situations when:

- You work with highly motivated people who admit they don't have all the answers.
- Your team members trust you as the coach.
- You support your team members while guiding them in their career goals.
- You work together with your team to define and facilitate the best strategies for both the team and the organization.
- You share the organization's mission, vision, and goals transparently with all team members.
- You invite them to join you in a quest for success.
- You facilitate everyone's progress toward the goals you've mutually set as well as toward organizational goals.

When you coach, you teach your people the ropes as necessary, acting as a mentor rather than an autocrat. You make suggestions in real time concerning what they can do to tweak their performance toward an optimum. When they don't quite reach a standard, you praise what they did right, then outline where you think they showed weakness and what they can do to improve. You provide the tools they need to succeed—because when they succeed, so do you.

Coaches create the kind of engaged, empowered employees needed for business survival today.

Reaching for Improvement

Today, workplace reality is undergoing a shift that's been coming on for decades. We see the technological innovations of the era combine with a desire for independence to bring employees and managers ever closer to each other on the employment continuum. No longer does the autocrat hold sway; a dictator is no longer needed all the time. Yes, leaders must have a firm hand occasionally, especially during crises and when dealing with green recruits. But otherwise, the coach has the upper hand over the autocrat in the drive toward excellence and a bountiful outcome.

The leader-as-coach provides the flexibility and agility businesses require on their road to success. Coaching also provides the motivation and confidence individual team members must feel to take you there. It seems a preordained conclusion that the importance of managing as a coach rather than an autocrat will increase in the foreseeable future.

If you haven't already started the shift yourself, it's time to begin.

BOOSTING ROI THROUGH LEARNING

Return on investment is as important in teams and individuals as it is for machines, buildings, and other tangible assets. Many people don't like this comparison because it equates human value to material wealth, yet it's been common in business for decades. Efficiency is a key component of producing good ROI.

But what comprises true efficiency in a useful business sense?

That's a question worth pursuing; the answer isn't necessarily what you might expect. Business "efficiency" has evolved beyond its classic dictionary definition, which is essentially minimizing the resources required to do something. That's fine as far as it goes—but what if the thing done right isn't the *right* thing? If your mechanic changes the wrong tire on your car, it doesn't matter how efficiently he does the job; you've still got a flat tire.

As Drucker said, "There is nothing so useless as doing efficiently that which should not be done at all." What we really want, then, is *effective* efficiency.

Running a Tight Ship

Maximizing personal and team productivity requires effective efficiency. As you strive in your efforts, ensure these activities get your attention:

1 **LEVERAGE TECHNOLOGY.** Embrace and encourage new trends, devices, and software as they appear. Let your workers use their own devices for business purposes if they want. Why not take advantage of a productivity source you don't have to pay for? Meanwhile, provide instant "anywhere" access to workplace information. Let team members work from alternate locations with Wi-Fi when it's practical. When a member of my office manager's family is ill, it's easy to let her work from home for the day, so she can still be productive. With Wi-Fi, Evernote, and all the snazzy apps

we have access to, workers can tap into work information no matter where they are. Give them a secure, reliable way to share ideas and communicate, allowing more flexibility and change-responsiveness.

2 **SET AND TRACK EFFICIENCY GOALS.** Once you've pared your ideas down to size and established goals with your team, set specific schedules for achievement. As with any project, break those goals into manageable pieces, each with its own milestones and deadlines. Once you've achieved a goal, retune and set a new one.

3 **MEASURE EVERYTHING.** You can better influence things when you can understand them, so keep an eye on all the metrics that matter for your team. Use an accountability system, project management software, SharePoint, a common spreadsheet on Google Docs, Outlook Task Assignments, or a scoreboarding system that tracks important team metrics. The systems you use can be off-the-shelf or proprietary—it doesn't matter as long as you use them consistently.

4 **BRAINSTORM REGULARLY.** Meet with your team periodically to exchange ideas on how best to achieve your strategic priorities and improve processes and procedures. Look for areas of overlap and eliminate redundancy. Discuss what your team is doing that doesn't provide value. Remove steps that no longer apply when a platform changes, and make sure each person documents everything, so a new person can get up to speed quickly. Remove your thought-filters and let your ideas cross-fertilize to see what kinds of interesting hybrids result. Consider concepts from other fields, and how they might apply to yours. What would you love to do if it were possible?

The Benefits of Consistent Training

For your team members to be productively efficient *and* effective, they need the right tools. This is an indispensable ROI tactic. (Yes, it's okay for tactics to be indispensable, even though people can't be.) Some personnel need blazing-fast computing power; others need smartphones and tablets that let them work on the go; still others might require specialized instruments to maximize their performance. Whatever the case, *all* of them need consistent training, undertaken as often as necessary to stay ahead of the changes rolling through your field.

No one wants to spend money if they don't have to. But remember: in business, what matters isn't what you spend *now*, but how much money you make *later*. You have to make short-term investments for long-term gain. It's all about ROI. Done correctly, training produces the extraordinary levels of ROI you need to stay ahead of the game.

Why Training Matters . . . and Works

- *Training improves confidence and therefore performance.* When people know they've been equipped to do their jobs properly, it boosts their spirits and reassures them they can achieve levels of competency and productivity they haven't realized in the past. Further, when employees understand why their work matters and how to do it, they're more likely to hit the mark or go above and beyond. While instructor-led classes are still popular, webinars and online learning are catching up. When the Montreal Transit System implemented an immersive e-Learning system, employee performance increased 32 percent, while training time decreased by 50 percent.[38]

- *Training saves the company money.* Well-trained employees make fewer errors and require less direct supervision. Furthermore, they spend less time thinking about problem solving, because they already know what to do. Consistent training also decreases employee turnover—a big drain on corporate costs.

- *Training earns the company money.* While money saved is equivalent to money earned, directly fattening the bottom line makes people sit up and take notice. A few years ago, Nations Hotel Company invested heavily in coaching and saw an ROI of 221 percent.[39]

- *Training increases employee productivity.* Motorola long since realized that every dollar invested in training can yield as much as a 30 percent gain in productivity within three years. That let the company cut costs by $3 billion and increase profits by 47 percent in 2000 alone.[40] According to another report—"The 2001 Global Training and Certification Study" by testing firms CompTIA and Prometric—as little as a 2 percent increase in productivity can result in a 100 percent increase in training ROI.[41]

  Researchers have consistently observed this effect over the years since. For example, Dillon Consulting, an international consulting firm, quadrupled its profits by 2009, after instituting a Project Management Training Program four years previously.[42] Similarly, in 2013, BSkyB, a top pay TV service in the UK and Ireland offering broadband and telephone services, reported a significant ROI after delivering 850,000 hours of training to its customer service representatives over a twelve-month period.[43]

Big-Time Payoff

Good, consistent training more than pays for itself in terms of employee confidence, performance, productivity, reduced turnover, and dollars earned on the bottom line. Rather than view it as a necessary evil, treat it as a positive expense—just as you would any initiative that promises to increase profits and benefit everyone all the way down the line.

Self-Care

Health

Acuity

TACTICAL WORK

12

BALANCE

Sustain Your Physical and Mental Health

In this last chapter, it all comes down to you and what you personally contribute to team productivity. In order to be an effective, efficient leader, you have to take care of yourself at least as well as you take care of your team, by maintaining balance in your life.

You might think that the need for a decent work/ life balance would be obvious to anyone, but white-collar workers tend to be more ambitious and driven than most. We forget that brainwork can be just as tiring as physical labor. We believe we can push ourselves longer than our blue-collar brethren, who are more likely to appreciate the need to decompress and recharge. Sometimes, this results in over-whelm, which can lead to a workflow breakdown you have to rebuild from. Such a recovery can take a while.

It's better not to go there in the first place! Don't work yourself to death; what's the point? Maintaining your health must be a priority if you want to sustain true, long-term productivity. Diet, exercise, sleep, taking enough rest breaks, and going on vacation when you should will keep you at the top of your game.

You especially have an obligation to take care of your mind, because mental acuity will help you achieve more than anything else. Some of this acuity will arise naturally from physical health, but, like even the best-forged blade, it can always use sharpening. Hone your neurons, keep up your spirits, and apply a mental whetstone to your wits to maximize your talents and therefore your productivity.

YOUR OWN SELF-CARE

These days, many in the white-collar world are just plain exhausted, stumbling along from one crisis to another and never getting the R&R they need. Let's suppose you've joined that trend, and your personal productivity has taken a nosedive. Maybe you've lost track of your planning process and your to-do lists have grown out of control. Perhaps you went on vacation and haven't been able to get on top of your inbox since. Could be you have a looming deadline you haven't even been able to think about. Or maybe unexpected changes in your industry have presented new challenges that have blown you off course.

Now what?

Every second you're out of the race, you and those depending on you fall further behind. So leap into action, resolved to restore your vitality in record time. But how do you revive your productivity? Do what you do when your computer crashes: a hard reboot.

Accept that you're stuck, stop wallowing in frustration, and hit Restart. But be warned—you may have to act harshly. When everything's ready, flip the proverbial switch and put your head down for a few hours to cut through the clutter and get back on track. Get mad. Get decisive. Get fast.

For me, a productivity hard reboot is a personal retreat. I check into a hotel a mile up the road and check out forty-eight hours later, refreshed, reenergized, and reorganized. I think, write, plan, strategize, and get caught up. I don't leave the room (it has a microwave and refrigerator, so I bring my meals with me). The process is so exciting, I can hardly sleep.

We can't control everything in our environment, but we *can* accept that things can and do fall apart. When they do, how you react will test your strength and character—and how quickly you bounce back. When you take it on the chin, bop life back and move on. Learn from experience, pull whatever's useful from the wreckage, and rebuild something stronger. Remember: you never really fail until you give up.

PRIORITIZING YOUR HEALTH

We certainly know we do better, more productive work when we feel well. And yet many of us get stuck in a vicious cycle. When we work long hours and run short on time, we cut into our precious free time—the time when we would do the things that keep us healthy: exercise, sleep, eat and drink properly, and have fun. Soon we find ourselves in an unproductive, unhealthy rut.

Clearly, productivity alone doesn't keep us healthy. In fact, the exact opposite is true. As psychotherapist Nathaniel Branden points out, "Productive achievement is a consequence and an expression of health and self-esteem, not its cause."

The Big Five

Good health doesn't automatically produce productivity, but it prepares you for it. You can't do your best work when you feel bad. You've noticed how sluggishly your brain works after a poor night's sleep or a missed meal, how distracting a growly stomach can be, and how low self-esteem can create nagging anxiety. Now compare all that to workdays when you felt in tip-top condition, bursting with energy and good health. I'll bet you performed extremely well on those days.

You can't control all the factors contributing to good health, but you *can* control most of them. I find these factors most important to me:

- *Sleep.* The typical adult requires seven to nine hours of restful sleep per night, though research supported by the National Sleep Foundation suggests, as of 2015, that some adults can get by on six under certain circumstances.[44] Among other things, sleep helps you fend off infection and illness, because your body does most of its cellular repairs while sleeping. Besides knitting up "the ravell'd sleave of care," as Shakespeare put it, sleep also forces you to stay in one spot while your muscles rest and recover. It lets your mind clear the slate and process what you've learned or experienced during the day. REM sleep helps you absorb new motor skills and gives your body the time to manufacture a steroid, DHEA, which keeps the wakefulness steroid, cortisol, in check. Good sleep may even help you maintain a desired weight. Sleep deprivation produces a natural appetite stimulant called ghrelin, while depressing the production of leptin, an appetite suppressant.[45] Therefore, the less you sleep, the hungrier you will be.

- *Eat well.* Maintaining a good diet is all about ensuring you get the nutrients needed to keep your personal productivity machine working without adding weight that will slow you down and drain your energy. Don't just count calories; balance protein, fats, and carbs, and be sure you get all the vitamins and minerals you need. *How* you eat is as important as *what* you eat. While you don't have to limit your diet to lettuce leaves and carrots at every meal, exercise portion control to keep your weight down, especially as you age and your metabolism slows.

- *Hydrate.* The human body consists mostly of water, so be sure to drink liquids throughout the day. But take care. Coffee, tea, and soda, while fine in moderation, contain caffeine—a diuretic that can pull water out of your system. To avoid calories, steer clear of sugary drinks as well. Keep a bottle of water on hand and take an occasional swallow throughout the day to make sure you're getting the water you need. While the "8 × 8" rule—eight eight-ounce glasses of water a day—may be a lot for you, drink at least a quart daily.

- *Exercise.* Ironically, the more active you are, the more energy you have. That's because exercise helps you keep your weight down and gets your blood pumping. Set an exercise routine you can stick to, whether it involves ten laps in the pool each morning, a brisk walk twice a day, or visiting the gym three times a week. Otherwise, sneak in subversive exercise: walk up stairs to the next floor to go to the restroom, do squats or leg lunges while talking on your hands-free phone, walk on your treadmill while you watch TV, park at the far end of the parking lot, and so on.

Microsoft's Mike Howard told me, "I invest the first hour of my day in exercise. I think that's important, because a healthy body equates also to a healthy mind. It gives you the endurance to deal with stress better and to manage the day better." I couldn't agree more.

- *Take care of your mental health.* Though some researchers argue you're more likely to succeed if your self-esteem isn't *too* high (thereby forcing you to constantly prove yourself), life is always easier when you're happy. Add pleasant things to your environment: an ego wall, pictures of family and pets, optimistic sayings, funny cartoons, plants, whatever it takes to keep your spirits high. Be sure to take your breaks—including vacations—and get serious about having fun.

It's All Connected

The Big Five are inextricably interrelated: sleep impacts weight as well as mental health, as do exercise and good diet; too much weight from poor diet and lack of exercise can contribute to self-esteem issues; happiness can convince you to take better care of yourself . . . you get the picture. Strive to get each of these factors under control, and your productivity will scale upward.

SHARPENING YOUR MENTAL ACUITY

Did you know that smart people actually think faster than "regular" people do? That's the conclusion of a 2009 twin study at UCLA that scanned specific parts of the brain using magnetic resonance imaging (MRI). The smarter the person, the faster the mental speed.[46]

For me, this begs the question: does being smart make you think faster, or does thinking faster make you smarter? The jury's still out on that, but I suspect it's a bit of both.

Either way, here are some suggestions that may help you boost your thinking speed:

1 FOCUS. By now, you know you can be more productive when you focus tightly on one issue to the exclusion of everything else. You can't keep it up indefinitely, but for an hour or so at a time, you can certainly hone in like a laser on what matters most. When you fall into a focus trance, you boost your thinking speed. I use a regular kitchen timer and set it for forty-five-minute focus sessions, which helps me get "in the zone."

2 TAKE ACTING CLASSES. I'll bet you didn't expect this one, but acting classes help you maintain your mental footing. I learned to think faster on my feet through improvisational exercises. They've helped my speaking ability in many ways: projecting confidence, maintaining poise when faced with a difficult audience member, and responding more quickly to questions. I've encouraged all three of my children to take drama classes and get used to performing in front of groups of people. Being fast on your feet will be especially helpful during challenging situations, such as in a sales presentation when the client is asking tough questions. If nothing else, the classes teach you how to respond to questions in ways that give you more time to answer.

3 EXERCISE YOUR MEMORY. Although your brain isn't a muscle, giving it a workout will help develop it. Your brain cells will forge new connections between each other, increasing speed of access to both information and reasoning ability. You'll find plenty of websites online to help you stretch your mental muscles, and there are logic puzzles galore that will keep your neurons active. New research suggests that crossword puzzles increase language fluency, but, contrary to popular belief, they don't develop your mind. If you like crosswords, try the tough British-style puzzles. With those, you have to figure out the clues before you can even guess the words.

4 **LEARN SOMETHING NEW . . . AND DO IT REPEATEDLY.** When you learn a new task, your brain rewires itself, often with interesting consequences. Not only do you learn more, but you may also develop shortcuts between neurons containing different information. When you repeat the task, it helps burn those new pathways into your neural network.[47] If necessary, start small and work your way up. Interestingly, exercise seems to help previously inactive Alzheimer's patients regain cognitive function;[48] maybe a new exercise routine can help you think faster when giving a business presentation.

5 **LEARN A NEW LANGUAGE.** This exposes you to a new way of thinking. Some linguists and neurologists believe our native languages establish our thought patterns for life.[49] If that's so, then studying a new language—especially one radically different from your own—can shake things up.

The Human Touch
The tips for improving mental acuity outlined here present a challenge: they take a lot of time and effort. Many people don't want to be bothered, because time's already in such short supply. But even the slightest increase in mental acuity will

serve you well. If you must pick and choose, at the very least, develop and maintain plenty of meaningful relationships in your life.

Spending time with family and friends can improve your mood and clear clogged mental pathways. Talking things out with others can help you frame your thoughts and process data, as extroverts can attest to. It can also help you relax— and that's when your subconscious mind takes over, grinding through problems and presenting solutions when you least expect them.

Lifting Your Spirits

While there are jobs that take place in harsh environments, if you're reading this book, I doubt yours is one of them. However, your environment may be sterile or uncomfortable. Poor working conditions can lead to decreased productivity and inferior performance. In particular, poor ergonomics can cause repetitive motion injuries. Addressing these issues costs less than paying worker's comp and losing productivity. Nowadays, desks have to be at the right height, computer screens at the right distance to avoid eyestrain, and keyboards easier to use.

How else can you make your office a better place to work? Here are six ways:

1 BRING A LITTLE OF THE OUTDOOR WORLD INSIDE.
Did you know that the air inside a building is often much more polluted than the outside air? As building materials age, they release gasses and particulates into the air. Limited air circulation may fail to remove these pollutants, as well as the dust, beverage and food odors, and other contaminants brought in. So what's one solution? Houseplants. In addition

to thriving on the carbon dioxide we exhale, many filter pollutants out of the air.[50] Some species, including mother-in-
law's tongue, don't even need much light to survive. Besides
all that, plants brighten up the place.

2 **THROW LIGHT ON THE SUBJECT.** Rather than close
yourself off from the outside world, open the blinds
to let the sunshine in. Your building probably already has
window films to cut down on harmful UV radiation, so it
can't hurt to be able to see outdoors. If you worry about
the motion or scenery distracting you, don't. It can actually
inspire you, and your plants can use the light. If it bothers
others, they can turn their back to it.

3 **SURROUND YOURSELF WITH THINGS THAT MAKE
YOU HAPPY.** A sterile cubicle does nothing to stimulate
productivity or maintain your sanity. Surround yourself with
things that make you happy. If your daughter's latest art project brings you joy, hang it on your wall. Fond of your cat?
Bring her picture to work. Encourage your people to follow
your lead and decorate as they will—as long as it doesn't get
in the way of their work—and provide the means to do so:
pushpins, tacks, magnets, etc. Content people do far better
work than overstressed worriers who wish they were anywhere except where they are.

4 **MAKE THE WORKPLACE MORE ATTRACTIVE.** A little
paint, prominently displayed team trophies, a Keurig and
plenty of K-cups in the break room, framed photos and art,
and serene decorative colors can make a huge difference in
how you and your team feel about your work. Soft curves
and rich woods liberally used in the office design and, to

quote Hemingway, "a clean, well-lighted place" in general will also make your working environment more pleasant.

5 **FIND/PROVIDE A PLACE TO BLOW OFF STEAM.** Google, one of the world's most innovative companies, provides places for stressed employees to go and have a little fun during their breaks. You too can provide interesting, well-equipped break rooms, attractively decorated courtyards, pleasant bathrooms, and well-maintained grounds for everyone's enjoyment.

6 **REMEMBER THAT "HAPPY IS AS HAPPY DOES."** If work were always tons of fun, we wouldn't call it work. But it doesn't have to be torture, either. If you do everything possible to tweak the enjoyment quotient a bit higher in the workplace, both you and your team members will be more willing to spend more time at work—and that will show in increased productivity and a better bottom line.

Less May Be More

No doubt about it: you have to keep your wits sharp to effectively lead a team. Fortunately, most of us get plenty of mental stimulation from the challenges of running that team and doing our job on a daily basis.

Think about it. In addition to juggling umpteen projects, you're constantly busy planning how to delegate them to your team members, trying to balance the summer's vacation schedule, digging up more work when times get lean, clearing workflow blockages, jump-starting new projects, mediating disputes between coworkers, introducing people to others in your network, and handling a hundred other tasks—while trying to do a little work on the side. That provides enough mental activity for any ten sudoku volumes, with a Martin Gardner book of math puzzles on the side.

So I'll buck the trend here and say that instead of doing *more* to hone your mental alertness, maybe you should do *less*.

The Inactivity Angle

My specialty as a productivity expert is showing people how to do more in less time. I practice what I preach and get a tremendous amount done. The most important part of my life revolves around my loved ones, so I want to spend as much time with them as possible.

But in a world where agility, flexibility, speed, and innovation have become watchwords, you can easily get overworked and overwhelmed. I believe doing too much causes you to *lose* your mental edge, *not* hone it.

You aren't a robot. You can't work nonstop. You must take a little time to back up, breathe—and give yourself a break. Literally. Then you can put your head down and get to work anew.

Try these tips to get you there:

1 **GET ON TOP OF YOUR TO-DO LISTS.** While you need to-do lists to structure your productivity, they can get out of hand. Triage mercilessly, then prioritize what remains by importance and due date. Practice purposeful abandonment of the least important tasks and delegate like crazy.

2 **REVIEW YOUR GOALS.** Stop, look around, and reevaluate where you are—and where you should be. Does your current path align with the organization's? What about your team and personal goals? If things seem hopelessly snarled, take a weekend off and check into a hotel for a forty-eight-

hour strategic thinking retreat as I do. You'll emerge organized and excited.

3 **TAKE YOUR BREAKS.** You have a lunch break and weekends off for a reason: to recharge your mental batteries, regaining your edge before you return to the front. You may occasionally need to skip a break or work through a weekend during crunch time, but don't make a habit of it. And take your full vacations! Escape the hassles of the office, if only for a week or two a year.

4 **DISCONNECT.** Stop checking work email during the evening. Be present with the people you care about most. Even if you stay busy physically, you still need a change that lets your brain bounce back to its normal elasticity and sharpness.

5 **HAVE FUN AT WORK.** Work doesn't have to mean drudgery. Don't be frivolous, but do give your team reasons to look forward to work every day. Do things to promote solidarity, celebrate important life events, and publically reward team members who've done exceptionally well.

Walking That Fine Line
Working hard and doing your job well are important; no one disputes that. That said, you shouldn't live to work.

Instead, you need to regain control of your productivity so you can get out of the office on time—not only to recharge and recapture your mental edge, but also to devote time to the people you care about and who care about you.

Sometimes work has to wait while you live the rest of your

life. Once you've taken your time off, for whatever reason, jump back into the fray when you're at your best. You'll end up doing a much better job than if you'd just trudged straight through.

Darren Smith of John Hancock Investments has struggled with this himself in the past. When asked how he's avoided burnout or workaholism, he replied,

> First, by clearly prioritizing the elements of my life that are most important and seeking to balance them on an overall basis. Also by realizing that business, and life, are not marathons, but instead are a series of sprints. With this realization, I find it much easier to summon the physical, emotional, and intellectual energy necessary to sprint with full energy and exertion when necessary, since I know that pace is temporary, and the effort necessary for this level of execution will not always be required.

Darren's advice is spot on. All it takes to do your job well without killing yourself is a few epiphanies like his. Keep them in mind and close to your heart.

CONCLUSION
The Evolving Business of Business

Few scholars have contributed more to business theory than
Peter F. Drucker, the Austrian-born management consultant
who turned the eye of a social scientist onto America's favorite
pastime—business. Business drives the engine of our progress
and has for more than a century.

With the publication of *The Effective Executive* in 1967,
Drucker codified the basics of modern business productivity.
He put into print the best of the strategies businesses had invented in the twentieth century to adapt to constantly shifting
technological and social change.

The Effective Executive has remained in print and constant use
since its publication almost fifty years ago, and rightly so. Few
business references have served us half as well. But half a century is a geological era in business terms, and though Drucker
updated his book through multiple editions, it's a bit dated
these days. Since his day, women have entered the business
field in unprecedented numbers, our world recently survived

the worst economic downturn since the Great Depression, and business technology has sprung far ahead of what even the most optimistic prophets predicted.

That's why I wanted to expand on Drucker's basic themes for the modern business arena. By no means do I intend to even *attempt* to unseat Drucker or imitate his work in any way; I just seek to supplement. My chapters don't map one-to-one with Drucker's, and there are almost twice as many. But I sought to bring many themes up to speed for the modern business era, where flexibility, agility, and on-the-spot, in-the-moment execution rule. On the website associated with this book, www.3TLeadership.com, I've included a personal journal, book club materials, and other resources to help you connect the dots between this volume and your own work.

These days, it's not enough for an executive to do the right things; he or she has to be superbly efficient, too. As executives, we must manage this intersection of efficiency and effectiveness carefully to ensure we do the right things *right*, wasting as little time as possible in the process.

We can no longer lock ourselves into a long-term plan of action; things change far too quickly for that to work. Even the most traditional corporations have set that concept aside in favor of dynamic, on-the-spot adaptation to the confusing modern business environment.

THE EVOLUTION TOWARD COMMON GROUND

Perhaps the greatest change we've seen while boldly going deeper into the Information Era is that the roles of manager and worker have evolved toward each other. These roles are no longer as strictly defined on either side of the equation, and the continuum between them is just that—a continuum, a smooth change from pure worker on one end to pure leader on the other.

This hasn't always been the case. Once upon a time, management was management, workers were workers, and never the twain met. Leadership was about autocracy, and workers weren't paid to think. Sure, a few stood on the rungs in between (like foremen). But even they remained workers, their roles well defined.

Today, an executive is anyone who executes strategy—from individual contributors through low-level management all the way to the C-Suite. The old roles have become blurry; one does what one has to, in the moment, to get things done. True managers lead these days by facilitating: that is, by making life easier for the rest of the team.

And leaders are team members, too, now more so than ever before. They're the ones who step up and clear the way for everyone else. While they may not often step in and do low-level tasks (it's not cost-efficient), they're still willing to roll up their sleeves and help when the team lacks the resources to achieve its tasks. Today's leader also leads by example, develops talent, and acts as an arbitrator when personalities clash.

INTO THE STORM

While it's difficult to predict a future in a dynamic field like business, Drucker often made predictions, many of which have come true.

His explication of the evolving role and value of knowledge workers, which he explored toward the end of his career, has proven solid in the years since. While manufacturing will always comprise a significant part of our economy, the white-collar world is where productivity will climb as older technologies mature and new ones appear.

It's hard to say what the next paradigm change may be. Though radio phones have been in use since World War II, cell phones and related advances in telephony weren't even a gleam in the eye of the marketplace when Drucker wrote *The Effective Executive*. Yet their contribution to the growth of productivity has been undeniable—that is, when we can eliminate *Schlimmbesserung* and compulsive technology addiction from the equation.

Knowledge work is decentralizing. Already, we're evolving away from the hive mentality. With low-cost Internet connections becoming ubiquitous, a world of outsourcing partners at our fingertips, and computer power doubling every eighteen months, we no longer have to collect in one place to do our work. In fact, telecommuting often makes more sense—though perhaps because it limits real-time control of the workforce and shatters preconceptions about how we should organize business, some executives see it as a threat.[51]

We know that honeybees congregate in hives to maximize their productivity. But few of us know about solitary mason bees, which are just as effective and efficient at pollinating plants, and may be the best honey producers.[52] Before long, I suspect, knowledge work like ours will move away from the hive mentality to the mason bee model. We can still work in teams, and we can still be superbly productive both individually and collectively. But in time, we'll all become executives as the roles of manager and worker merge.

Corporate structures will simplify and, while they'll still be profitable and just as amenable to growth and development as ever, the component parts—the individual knowledge workers—will be more independent. This is a good thing. Like the distributed nature of cloud networks, a decentralized work-force ensures that shared culture and projects are spread out over so many components that nothing can easily destroy them—natural disasters, accidents, wars, or terrorist attacks.

My intentions for this book were to outline and update the practices effective leaders should follow to manage their time well in 2020 and beyond.

We'll have to wait a few decades to see if my vision was 20/20 in its perception of how things continue to change. If nothing else, I feel that we all have to learn to be effective, efficient leaders—because all knowledge workers will almost certainly need these skills going forward.

Thank you for reading this book. I look forward to hearing from you.

▶▶ Keep the momentum going and continue to develop your time management skills after reading this book! Visit **www.3TLeadership.com** for free related resources, including a personal journal to take notes as you read, a discussion guide to share with your leadership team, and video lessons to review key learning points.

NOTES

1. Adam Hartung, "Hostess' Twinkie Defense Is a Management Failure," *Forbes Online*, November 18, 2012, http://www.forbes .com/sites/adamhartung/2012/11/18/hostess-twinkie-defense-is-a -management-failure; and Susan Adams, "Why Hostess Had to Die," *Forbes Online*, November 21, 2012, http://www.forbes.com/sites /susanadams/2012/11/21/why-hostess-had-to-die/.
2. Richard Dobbs, Jaana Remes, Sven Smit, James Manyika, Jonathan Woetzel, and Yaw Agyenim-Boateng, "Urban World: The Shifting Global Business Landscape," *McKinsey Global Institute Report*, October 2013, http://www.mckinsey.com/Insights/Urbanization/ Urban_world_The_shifting_global_business_landscape?cid=other -eml-alt-mgi-mck-oth-1310.
3. Richard Branson, "Richard Branson on Managing Change," *Entrepreneur Magazine*, January 23, 2011, http://www.entrepreneur.com /article/217944.
4. Laura Northrup, "Same Crew Demolished Wrong House Two Days in a Row," *Consumerist*, August 23, 2013, http://consumerist .com/2013/08/23/same-crew-demolished-wrong-house-two-days -in-a-row/.
5. Clive Thompson, "Learn to Let Go: How Success Killed Duke Nukem," *Wired*, December 21, 2009, http://www.wired.com/2009 /12/fail_duke_nukem/.
6. Jason Schreier, "How LucasArts Fell Apart," *Kotacu.com*, September 27, 2013, reprinted April 13, 2015, http://kotaku.com/how-lucasarts -fell-apart-1401731043.

7. Nina Munk, *Fools Rush In: Steve Case, Jerry Levin, and the Unmaking of AOL Time Warner* (New York: HarperBusiness, 2005).

8. Vincent Barraba, *The Decision Loom: A Design for Interactive Decision-Making in Organizations* (New York: Triarchy Press, 2011). Barraba is a former Kodak executive.

9. "The Last Kodak Moment?" *The Economist,* January 14, 2012, http://www.economist.com/node/21542796.

10. Chunka Mui, "How Kodak Failed," *Forbes Online,* January 18, 2012, http://www.forbes.com/sites/chunkamui/2012/01/18/how-kodak -failed/3/.

11. Sam Gustin, "The Fatal Mistake That Doomed Blackberry," *Time Online,* September 24, 2013, http://business.time.com/2013/09/24 /the-fatal-mistake-that-doomed-blackberry/.

12. Simon Collinson and Melvin Jay, "Complexity Kills Profits—CEOs Need to Simplify Their Businesses," *The European Business Review,* November 24, 2011, http://www.europeanbusinessreview.com /?p=3105.

13. Josh Sanburn, "5 Reasons Borders Went Out of Business (and What Will Take Its Place)," *Time Online,* July 19, 2011, http://business .time.com/2011/07/19/5-reasons-borders-went-out-of-business -and-what-will-take-its-place/.

14. Ibid.

15. Josh Sanburn, "E-Books: Why Barnes & Noble Avoided Borders' Fate," *Time Online,* March 18, 2011, http://content.time.com/time /business/article/0,8599,2057760,00.html.

16. Lee Tyler, "Amazon Kindle Fire Unveiled," *Ubergizmo.com,* September 28, 2011, http://www.ubergizmo.com/2011/09/amazon-kindle -fire-unveiled/.

17. Dina Spector, "The 11 Biggest Food Flops of All Time," *Business Insider Online,* January 20, 2012, http://www.businessinsider.com /food-failures-2012-1?op=1.

18. Ann Thayer, "What's That Stuff? Silly Putty," *Chemical and Engineering News* 78, no. 48 (November 27, 2000): 27, http://pubs.acs .org/cen/whatstuff/stuff/7848scit3.html.

19. Ron Hunter, *Toy Box Leadership: Leadership Lessons from the Toys You Loved as a Child* (Nashville, Tenn.: Thomas Nelson, 2010).

20. Peter Werder and Philippe Rothlin, *Diagnose Boreout* (Munich, Germany: Redline Wirtschaft, 2007).

21. "Survey Finds Balanced Workload Is Best, but Underworked Employees Are Least Happy," *PRNewswire,* December 20, 2009, http://www.prnewswire.com/news-releases/survey-finds-balanced -workload-is-best-but-underworked-employees-are-least-happy -75894882.html.

22. Dobbs et al., "Urban World."

23. Clifton Fadiman and Andre Bernard, *Bartlett's Book of Anecdotes* (New York: Little, Brown, 2000), 210.

24. Alex Taylor, "Leading the Way: Leadership Should Be Substance over Style," *The Gazette* (Cedar Rapids, Iowa), August 11, 2013, http://thegazette.com/2013/08/11/leading-the-way-leadership -should-be-substance-over-style.

25. Rod Collins, *Wiki Management: A Revolutionary New Model for a Rapidly Changing and Collaborative World* (New York: ANACOM, 2013), 120–121.

26. Don MacPherson, "The Results Are In," Modern Survey, March 29, 2013, http://www.modernsurvey.com/blog/the-results-are-in.

27. Modern Survey, "The State of Employee Engagement—Fall 2014," http://www.modernsurvey.com/wp-content/uploads/2014/11 /The-State-of-Engagement-Report-Fall-2014.pdf.

28. MacPherson, "The Results Are In."

29. Eric Markowitz, "7 Unusual Ways to Motivate Your Employees," *Inc.*, http://www.inc.com/ss/7-unusual-ways-motivate-employees.

30. MacPherson, "The Results Are In"; Modern Survey, "The State of Employee Engagement."

31. Jillian D'Onfro, "The Truth about Google's Famous '20% Time' Policy," *Business Insider,* April 17, 2015, http://www.businessinsider .com/google-20-percent-time-policy-2015-4.

32. Vivian Giang, "A New Report Ranks America's Biggest Companies Based On How Quickly Employees Jump Ship," *Business Insider,* July 25, 2013, http://www.businessinsider.com/companies-ranked -by-turnover-rates-2013-7.

33. Robert A. Eckert, "The Two Most Important Words," *Harvard*

Business Review, April 2013, https://hbr.org/2013/04/the-two-most-important-words; and 100 Best Companies to Work For Archive, 2006–2013, *Fortune,* http://archive.fortune.com/magazines/fortune/best-companies/2013/list/.

34. Armin Falk and Urs Fischbacher, "A Theory of Reciprocity," *Games and Economic Behavior* 54, no. 2 (February 2006): 293–315, http://www.sciencedirect.com/science/article/pii/S0899825605000254.

35. Alexander Pope, "An Essay on Man," archived on Project Gutenberg, August 20, 2007, http://www.gutenberg.org/files/2428/2428-h/2428-h.htm.

36. Richard Saul Wurman, *Information Anxiety* (New York: Doubleday, 1987).

37. Jonathan B. Spira, "Leadership in an Age of Information Overload," *Overload Stories,* July 28, 2011, http://www.overloadstories.com/2011/07/leadership-io/.

38. Steve Wexler, Kevin Corti, Anne Derryberry, Clark Quinn, and Angela van Barneveld, *Immersive Learning Simulations 2008* (Santa Rosa, Calif.: The eLearning Guild, 2008).

39. Jack J. Phillips, "The ROI in Business Coaching: A Real-Life Example," Association for Talent Development, March 14, 2006, https://www.td.org/Publications/Newsletters/Links/2006/03/The-ROI-in-Business-Coaching-a-Real-Life-Example.

40. Tim Lane, "Learning to Succeed in Business with Information Technology," Motorola, 2000.

41. CompTIA and Prometric. "The 2001 Global Training and Certification Study," CompTIA, 2001.

42. Lynette Gillis and Allan Bailey, "Measuring the ROI of Project Management Training" (case study), Centre for Learning Impact, Canada, 2009, http://c.ymcdn.com/sites/www.cstd.ca/resource/resmgr/iip/dillon_report_final_english.pdf.

43. Amy Bell, "BSkyB—Driven by Customer Service Excellence," The Institute of Customer Service, March 20, 2013, https://www.instituteofcustomerservice.com/12103-10841/BSkyB---Driven-by-customer-service-excellence.html.

44. "How Much Sleep Do We Really Need?" National Sleep Foundation, 2015, http://sleepfoundation.org/how-sleep-works/how-much-sleep-do-we-really-need.

45. F.P. Cappuccio, F.M. Taggart, N.B. Kandala, A. Currie, E. Peile, S. Stranges, and M.A. Miller, "Meta-analysis of Short Sleep Duration and Obesity in Children, Adolescents and Adults," *Sleep* 31, no. 5 (2008): 619–626; University of Warwick, "Sleep Deprivation Doubles Risks of Obesity in Both Children and Adults," *ScienceDaily*, July 13, 2006, http://www.sciencedaily.com/releases /2006/07/060713081140.htm; Karine Spiegel, Esra Tasali, Plamen Penev, and Eve Van Cauter, "Brief Communication: Sleep Curtailment in Healthy Young Men Is Associated with Decreased Leptin Levels, Elevated Ghrelin Levels, and Increased Hunger and Appetite," *Annals of Internal Medicine* 141, no. 11 (2004): 846–850; and Shahrad Taheri, Ling Lin, Diane Austin, Terry Young, Emmanuel Mignot, "Short Sleep Duration Is Associated with Reduced Leptin, Elevated Ghrelin, and Increased Body Mass Index," *PLoS Medicine* 1, no. 3 (2004): e62, doi:10.1371/journal.pmed.0010062.

46. Ming-Chang Chiang, Marina Barysheva, David W. Shattuck, Agatha D. Lee, Sarah K. Madsen, Christina Avedissian, Andrea D. Klunder, Arthur W. Toga, Katie L. McMahon, Greig I. de Zubicaray, Margaret J. Wright, Anuj Srivastava, Nikolay Balov, and Paul M. Thompson, "Genetics of Brain Fiber Architecture and Intellectual Performance," *Journal of Neuroscience* 29, no. 7 (February 18, 2009): 2212–2224.

47. Denise C. Park, Jennifer Lodi-Smith, Linda Drew, Sara Haber, Andrew Hebrank, Gérard N. Bischof, and Whitley Aamodt, "The Impact of Sustained Engagement on Cognitive Function in Older Adults," *Psychological Science* 25, no. 1 (2014): 103–112, http:// pss.sagepub.com/content/early/2013/11/07/0956797613499592 .abstract?papetoc.

48. J. Carson Smith, Kristy A. Nielson, Piero Antuono, Jeri-Annette Lyons, Ryan J. Hanson, Alissa M. Butts, Nathan C. Hantke, Matthew D. Verber, "Semantic Memory Functional MRI and Cognitive Function after Exercise Intervention in Mild Cognitive Impairment," *Journal of Alzheimer's Disease* 37, no. 1 (2013): 197–215; University of Maryland, "Exercise May Be the Best Medicine for Alzheimer's Disease," *ScienceDaily*, July 30, 2013, www.sciencedaily .com/releases/2013/07/130730123249.htm.

49. Lera Boroditsky, "Does Language Shape Thought?: Mandarin and

English Speakers' Conceptions of Time," *Cognitive Psychology* 43 (2001): 1–22; Robert B. Kaplan. "Cultural Thought Patterns in Inter-Cultural Education," *Language Learning* 16 (1966): 1–20.

50. B.C. Wolverton, Willard L. Douglas, and Keith Bounds, "A Study of Interior Landscape Plants for Indoor Air Pollution Abatement" (report), NASA, July 1, 1989, https://archive.org/details/nasa _techdoc_19930072988.

51. Jill Krasny, "Yahoo CEO: Why I Was Right about Telecommuting," *Inc.,* May 28, 2013, http://www.inc.com/jill-krasny/marissa -mayer-twitter-telecommuting-policy.html.

52. Margriet Dogterom, *Pollination with Mason Bees: A Gardener and Naturalists' Guide to Managing Mason Bees for Fruit Production* (Coquitlam, B.C., Canada: Beediverse Publishing, 2002).

ACKNOWLEDGMENTS

After twenty-five years of being a professional speaker, productivity enthusiast, and seven-time book author, I'm keenly
aware that some of you have never heard of me before reading
this book. So by way of introduction, I thought I'd share the
answers to the three most common questions I'm asked.

The first question is, "How did you become a speaker?"
For me, it was a process of elimination. I always wanted to
be a performer. When I was five years old, I used to tape
record myself singing "You Are My Sunshine," "The Rain-
bow Connection," and "Wendy." My mother would play
the tapes for me in the car as she drove, which must have
made her crazy, but it kept me occupied until we reached
our destination. My first public debut was playing "Ngana"
in *South Pacific* when I was eight years old. I sang, danced,
and acted my way through school. But then my ballet teacher
told me my legs weren't long or thin enough for me to make
it big. My voice coach told me I had a nice voice, but I'd
never make it on Broadway. My acting coach told me I was
good, but I wasn't cut out for Hollywood.

Then I saw Zig Ziglar present at a motivational rally when
I was fourteen years old. As we were leaving, one of my

friends turned to me and said, "You could do that!" From that point forward, I wanted to *be* Zig Ziglar. I said to myself, "Hey, a little song and dance, a lot of acting, and I get to be in front of an audience. Perfect!" That's where I first learned about professional speaking.

The second question people ask me is, "How did you pick your topic of productivity?" I grew up on the US Air Force Academy in Colorado Springs, Colorado. My father, USAF Retired Colonel Kenneth Wenker, holds a PhD in Philosophy, which meant you had to develop the gift of gab if you ever wanted to get a word in edgewise at the dinner table.

The military and my father taught me the foundation of my presentations today: discipline, order, planning, structure, accountability, and perseverance. Even as a young girl, I had "systems." My stuffed animals lived on my bed in a specific order during the day and on my toy box in another specific order at night. I never left the house without making my bed. I actually folded and put my clothes away. I made to-do lists and had files. I had a precise order in which I got dressed, brushed my teeth, and brushed my hair. My mom said I was the kid on the playground in kindergarten looking at my watch and instructing, "Okay everyone . . . we have fifteen minutes . . . let's play!"

Fast forward through an MBA at twenty-one, the youngest ever at the University of Colorado at that time, I was told. People started asking me, "How did you get your MBA at twenty-one?" so I started giving little talks. And the rest, as they say, is history. After several years in corporate America, I started my own business in 1992, taught at several universities, and became a CareerTrack speaker, traveling around the country giving public seminars. Then I started working with my own private clients.

That leads to the third question I'm asked, which is, "How did you create a successful business?" That's an easy answer: the amazing family, friends, mentors, and partners in my life.

The most important people in my life are my incredible husband, John, and my three children, Meagan, Johnny, and James. Thank you so much for your tolerance of my crazy travel schedule and your undying support. I love you all so much. My gratitude also goes to my mother-in-law, Eileen Stack, who supports our family with her time in countless ways.

I'm grateful for my colleagues in my two mastermind groups, the Expert Speakers Network and the Elite Retreat. I appreciate my professional speaker colleagues, fellow members of the National Speakers Association, who are like an extended family. I fly more than 100,000 miles a year and spend a lot of time in hotels, so this business can get quite lonely. My NSA friendships make life fun and interesting. I was privileged to be NSA's president in 2011–2012 and am especially honored to have been recently inducted into the *Speaker Hall of Fame®*, of which Zig Ziglar was a member.

Mentors like Dianna Booher (to whom I dedicated my book *Execution IS the Strategy*), Connie Podesta, and Kathy Cooperman (to whom I dedicated this book) have helped me grow, and I am thankful for your time and caring. Mark Sanborn is also a steadfast friend and mentor, whom I also appreciate for being married to my dear friend Darla.

People always ask me how I stay so organized, given my hectic schedule. The secret is to have an incredible team of people surrounding you. Thank you to Jin Voelkelt, my office manager; Christine Page, my business manager; Becca Fletcher, my marketing manager; and Lance Gibb, my technology manager. They are the grease that keeps the machine running smoothly in my life, and I simply wouldn't be able to function without them!

Thanks to the entire team at Berrett-Koehler, and especially to my editor Neal Maillet, for his continued enthusiastic support of my work. Another big thanks goes to the independent reviewers whose eagle eyes and creative ideas helped make this book better: Floyd Largent, Barbara McNichol, Simon Blattner, Gauri Reyes, and Pam Gordon.

Last but certainly not least, I thank my clients, my audiences, and YOU, my readers. Your enthusiasm for my work keeps me curious about the world of productivity. I am truly grateful for your support. By sharing the answers to those three questions, I hope you got to know me a bit.

There's one last question that I always ask myself, which is, "How did I get so blessed?"

I simply thank the Lord.

INDEX

ABOUT THE AUTHOR

Laura Stack is an award-winning keynote speaker, bestselling author, and leading expert in the field of human performance and workplace issues. She is the president of The Productivity Pro, Inc., which specializes in productivity improvement in high-stress organizations.

Laura has authored numerous productivity books, which have been published in more than twenty countries. She writes on improving productivity, lowering stress, and saving time in her columns in *The Business Journal*, *Huffington Post*, *Productive*, and *Time Management*. Laura holds the Certified Speaking Professional (CSP) designation from the National Speakers Association and was inducted into the exclusive CPAE *Speaker Hall of Fame®*. She was the 2011–2012 President of the National Speakers Association.

Laura has been featured in the *New York Times*, *USA Today*, *Wall Street Journal*, *Entrepreneur*, and *Forbes* magazine. She has been a spokesperson for Microsoft, Dannon, belVita, 3M, Skillsoft, Office Depot, Day-Timer, and Xerox. Her client list features top Fortune 500 companies, including P&G, Cisco Systems, Toyota, Walmart, Aramark, Bank of America, Wells Fargo, and Time Warner, plus government agencies such as the Internal Revenue Service, the United States Air Force Academy, the Census Bureau, and the US Senate.

For twenty-five years, Laura's keynote speeches and seminars have provided audiences with immediately actionable ideas on time and stress management, life balance, and execution. She uses both high energy and high content to educate, entertain, and motivate audiences to produce greater results in the workplace. Laura's live presentations include:

What to Do When There's Too Much to Do (burnout and life balance)
Doing the Right Things Right (leadership and time management)
Execution IS the Strategy (team and employee productivity)
Attack of the Productivity Suckers! (focus and productivity)
Managing Your Time, Tasks, and Email (workflow and Outlook)

For more information on bringing Laura or a Certified Productivity Pro Consultant (CPPC) to your organization, visit www.TheProductivityPro.com or call The Productivity Pro, Inc. at 303-471-7401.

GOING FURTHER

If you have found *Doing the Right Things Right* valuable,
you might explore the following:

Books and Other Resources
What to Do When There's Too Much to Do; details at:
    www.TheProductivityPro.com/whattodo
Execution IS the Strategy; details at: www.ExecutionIsThe
    Strategy.com
Other books, CDs, DVDs, self-study audio, video training,
    MP3s, etc.: www.TheProductivityPro.com/products-page

Microsoft Outlook Expertise
Microsoft Outlook twelve-hour online video training:
    www.TheProductivityPro.com/Outlook
Microsoft Outlook Tips and Tricks: www.TheProductivity
    Pro.com/Laura

Tips
Weekly one-minute personal productivity video training
    series "The Productivity Minute": www.TheProductivity
    Minute.com/
Weekly productivity bulletin, The Productivity Pro®:
    www.TheProductivityPro.com/subscribe

Social Media
Facebook: www.facebook.com/productivitypro
LinkedIn: www.linkedin.com/in/laurastack
Twitter: www.twitter.com/laurastack
YouTube: www.youtube.com/theproductivitypro

Additional Articles and Assessments
Blog: www.TheProductivityPro.com/blog
Free articles for download: www.TheProductivityPro.com/articles
Self-assessments from Laura's books: www.TheProductivity
    Pro.com/quizzes

Berrett–Koehler
Publishers

Connecting people and ideas
to create a world that works for all

Dear Reader,

Thank you for picking up this book and joining our worldwide community of Berrett-Koehler readers. We share ideas that bring positive change into people's lives, organizations, and society.

To welcome you, we'd like to offer you a free e-book. You can pick from among twelve of our bestselling books by entering the promotional code BKP92E here: http://www.bkconnection.com/welcome.

When you claim your free e-book, we'll also send you a copy of our e-newsletter, the *BK Communiqué*. Although you're free to unsubscribe, there are many benefits to sticking around. In every issue of our newsletter you'll find

- A free e-book
- Tips from famous authors
- Discounts on spotlight titles
- Hilarious insider publishing news
- A chance to win a prize for answering a riddle

Best of all, our readers tell us, "Your newsletter is the only one I actually read." So claim your gift today, and please stay in touch!

Sincerely,

Charlotte Ashlock
Steward of the BK Website

Questions? Comments? Contact me at bkcommunity@bkpub.com.

MIX
Paper from
responsible sources
FSC® C002589

Certified

Corporation
bcorporation.net